FULL BODY PRESENCE

Gestalt in house 7/09

Dorothy Charles

The Healing Relationship)

1. The facilitator has to demonstrate that he/she is trustworthy, non-judgmental + compassionate

2. The facilitator must be present, attentive, + understands what the client is experiencing moment to moment.

These qualities are lived, embodied, + demonstrated.

The ability to focus on another is a non-egocentric state of being.

The personal + spiritual development of the facilitator is essential.

What is the source of nourishment, grounding that supports this state in you?

Full Body Presence

Explorations, Connections, and More
to Experience Present Moment Awareness

Suzanne Scurlock-Durana

RESTON, VIRGINIA

Published in the United States by
Healing from the Core Media
www.fullbodypresence.com

Editor:
Ja-lene Clark

Photo of Suzanne Scurlock-Durana:
Amelia Mitchell

Cover, text design, and illustrations:
David Andor / www.wavesource.com.au

Illustrations based on original designs by:
Kay Hansen

May you arouse your
Wholehearted listening body and
Receive the news of the universe
That is singing all around us.

May we join with those throughout this world,
Visible and invisible, who tend—with heart—
The indigenous soul and beauty of this world.

From *Blessing* by Susan Harper 2006
Continuum Montage

TABLE OF CONTENTS

∿

Foreword

~

I have known Suzanne since 1983, when she took one of my first CranioSacral Therapy classes and then told me she wanted to teach for me. In the 25 years since then, I have had the pleasure of working with her and experiencing her nurturing support and open-hearted approach to life. While she is one of our original instructors at The Upledger Institute, her passion has clearly been in the work she is now presenting here in *Full Body Presence*.

This book can be an important message to all of us in healthcare and anyone who is in a care-giving role. Our instructors, our clinicians, the parents and families of the patients we see here at The Upledger Clinic—every one of them can benefit by learning how to stay energetically grounded and full, with healthy boundaries that allow them to connect deeply, without burning out.

This is the concept Suzanne brings to all of us. Her curiosity and willingness to be open to discovery have led her around the globe and back again to what she delivers in this instruction manual on how to stay calm and centered under all kinds of life stressors. She has gathered skills from the many disciplines she has studied, and she has distilled them here in a methodology that is simple, straightforward, effective, and practical.

Through *Full Body Presence*, her work now has the opportunity to reach out into the world in a big way. It can support what we do every day with our CranioSacral Therapy patients. We help them connect more fully to themselves. Suzanne's work can then help them address the challenges they might face when they leave our offices and return to their lives. They can maintain healthy boundaries, stay grounded and speak their truth, and replenish themselves when life takes it out of them.

You'll discover that process right here in this book, which shows you how to be friends with your body—how to relate to it as an ally rather than something to control, judge, manipulate, or push away. In short, how to achieve your own full body presence.

So, as Suzanne would say...enjoy!

John Upledger, D.O., O.M.M.

Note from the Editors

∼

Author's Definitions of
Full Body Presence Terminology

As a guide for living with full body presence, it is necessary to begin by defining certain terms because we are giving language here to states of conscious awareness and presence not previously discussed in this way. Memorization of these terms is not required, as you will learn much more about each of them throughout this book. Please read the definitions now, and then refer back to this section as needed.

Full Body Presence: the ability to feel all parts of your body, with a good flow of healthy energy moving through you. It also includes a connection to your inner and outer healthy resources and a good sense of healthy boundaries. Full body presence is the foundation of a strong, therapeutic presence.

Disrupted Body Presence: impaired ability to sense or feel certain parts of your body due to physical or emotional trauma, disease, exhaustion, stress, sensory disorganization, or cultural or religious rules about body awareness. Most people have some degree of disrupted body presence in any given moment due to life's stressors and demands as well as from any of the factors mentioned above.

Grounding: the skill of being able to connect through your feeling senses—in a visceral way—to the earth under you or any other healthy energy resource. In this book, the focus is on grounding into, or connecting with, unconditional, healthy resources.

Healthy Resources: the resources which are life-enhancing and replenishing, such as; connections with nature that are rejuvenating, a memory that is reassuring or empowering, nutritious foods, nurturing touch, a loving relationship, or a satisfying, creative endeavor.

Unhealthy Connections: connections that are draining or life-taking. Unhealthy connections might involve addictive substances like drugs and cigarettes, or habits like excessive alcohol consumption, overeating, compulsive gambling, or mindless shopping. Such connections may also involve relationships with people who are unreliable or conditional, such as controlling parents who berate you if you don't take their advice, co-workers who take advantage of you rather than support you, or lovers who betray or abuse you.

Healthy Boundary: your skin generally defines your physical boundary, which is not to be crossed by anyone without your permission. This boundary is the awareness of where you stop and the rest of the world begins. A healthy boundary allows nurturing resources in and filters out what is life-taking or draining. It gives you the power to say "yes" or "no" to those who want to cross your boundaries. A healthy emotional boundary does not accept words or energy directed your way that is not appropriate or healing.

Container: a metaphor for your body that gives you a sense of personal boundaries. Your energy field and all that your body is comprised of naturally reside in your container.

Internal Landscape: describes your inner world, including sensations, images, emotions, messages, and subtle cues that inform and develop your body's innate intelligence.

Navigational System: a metaphor for your body's natural capacity to discern and track what is happening internally and externally. From the information received through the navigational system of your body, you can make more aware, informed, intelligent decisions. This allows you to take action in your life, to navigate, from inside yourself.

Energetic Awareness: the ability to recognize and interpret sensory information and subtle cues in your body and in the environment. Your energetic awareness is an integral part of your internal landscape and navigational system.

Therapeutic Presence: the capacity to hold a healing space for another by your calm, centered quality of being. This presence amplifies the effectiveness of whatever technical skills you already have and also maximizes treatment outcomes. It is a quality of *being,* a rapport, that feels healing, steady, and safe.

Introduction

∼

AS A CHILD, I was fascinated by the invisible energy dynamics that connect us all. Growing up on the front pew of a Baptist Church, as a preacher's daughter, I was constantly immersed in the warm river of resonant vibration, from the rich gospel singing to my father's powerful, benevolent presence.

I remember one night at age ten. I was standing alone outside the church in the warm, lush darkness of a Washington, D.C. summer, after a particularly vibrant singing service. Even though everything was over and the night was quiet, my insides were still buzzing.

Suddenly I felt, arising from inside my body, a deep surge of connection with all of the nature around me—the tall oaks, the earth, the night sky. The stars were suddenly very close to me. I felt huge and tiny all at the same time. Tears of unexplainable joy welled up from deep within my belly. With this feeling of oneness came a sense of belonging and presence. I felt filled up and at peace with the world. My only thought was, "This is the way I was meant to be."

For the next few days this sense of fullness and belonging lingered in my body. I noticed that the world felt friendlier. It was easier to be a kind big sister. It was easier to live by the dictates to "love thy neighbor" that I was learning in Sunday school.

That was my first conscious taste of directly experiencing the deep flow of life energy that we all have available to us—the connection that fills us up and makes true compassion possible—the connection that brings us into the moment and naturally feeds our sense of full body presence.

Almost everyone has experienced moments or had sacred encounters of this kind. It might be an experience of deep connectedness when holding a newborn, the wind in your face as you look out over a breathtaking mountain vista, being held safely in the arms of your beloved, or a moment of grace in meditation or prayer—the sense of being fully present can come in all kinds of ways.

Within a few weeks of my experience, that feeling of oneness and full body presence dissipated and became a distant memory. This diminishment of our full body presence inevitably happens to us all to one degree or another, depending on our circumstances. Some of us barely have a chance to experience what it is like to be free, to inhabit our bodies, to have a sense of oneness, to learn to trust ourselves and be comfortable in the world. We can get caught up in the "cultural trance": in other's expectations, in busy-ness, in fear and anger and doubt.

The experience on that warm summer night when I was ten, as well as other similar experiences that were to follow, led me to become deeply interested in the process of being more fully present in each moment of my life. This led me to study and practice yoga, T'ai Chi, Qi Gong, meditation, and Native American spiritual traditions.

For the last 25 years, I have been bringing this experience to others through my work as a practitioner and teacher of CranioSacral therapy and other related bodywork modalities—

helping others to access their own internal aliveness.

What I learned during that time as a student and a teacher is that when we have the skills to *drop directly into sensation within our bodies,* and let the mind become our ally—simply noticing without judgment what is going on inside ourselves—the path to present moment awareness opens before us.

To clarify and guide this opening to present moment awareness, I distilled a group of principles from all my studies and practices. I now refer to these as the Five Principles of Full Body Presence. These principles will help you discern what you need most to heal and grow. They are important indicators in your internal navigational system. They inform you of when you are most present and when your presence is disrupted in some way. You can then choose to move in a more life-giving direction.

The mission of *Full Body Presence* is to help you access your connection to your own body and life energy so that you enjoy each present moment more fully. This is your birthright. It is for your personal growth, creativity, and wellbeing, *and* so that you can be a source of support for others and for the greater good of the community. It has been my experience that when people find their inner gifts and use them, everyone benefits.

Many of the key elements of *Full Body Presence* have grown out of my teaching healthcare professionals a hands-on healing system called CranioSacral therapy. This system demands that its practitioners learn to listen acutely with all of their senses and to develop an ability to tune into the subtle physical and energy cues of the person on their therapy table.

Many of my students come to me with years of clinical experience. Many have mastered the manual and intuitive skills needed to work with clients effectively, yet few know how to hold a strong, healing *presence* for another person.

They are hungry to know how to develop this *therapeutic presence*—to remain grounded in the face of the strong client emotions often evoked in the healing process; to be deeply empathetic without taking on their client's pain, grief or rage, or without being triggered emotionally themselves; to facilitate the healing process without inadvertently violating the client's boundaries or losing their own.

Often practitioners have this knowledge *intuitively*; yet rarely know *consciously* what they are doing so that they can apply the same principles and energetic awareness skills in other areas of their lives.

Those skills and principles are taught in this book and audio and will provide you with the capacity to hold a strong therapeutic presence, without burning out. In fact, in using these tools you will probably find that you have *more* energy for *all* areas of your life.

Full Body Presence is an abridged version of what I have been teaching and developing for more than 20 years in the Healing From the Core training series—custom-tailored here for individual, self-directed use. A central part of *Full Body Presence* is the audio version of the *Explorations*. These *Explorations* differ from other self-help book "guided imagery techniques" and meditations in that they invite you to nourish, strengthen, and explore your *unique* internal landscape through developing an increasing awareness of *your* body. These are not affirmations or prescriptions. They are, in essence, an energetic awareness-building practice. One through which you can integrate body, mind, and spirit, connecting with your deep inner knowing. Thus reclaiming your innate energy, resilience, and direction.

This book is meant to be read straight through without

jumping around. If you find a chapter that feels familiar, simply skim it—but please read it *all* because the skills taught here build on each other. Every chapter and *Exploration* has a distinct purpose. The *Explorations* build on each other, so please initially listen to the audio *Explorations in order*. Listening to the audio portion of this book is central to this material. Simply reading the transcripts in the back of the book will not convey the information fully.

Please follow the lead I am offering you here. I have taken thousands of people through this process with amazing results. Get out your CD player or download the audio now so that you can listen to it easily when the time comes. Enjoy!

Chapter 1

∿

Out of
Touch

O UR BODIES are the containers for our spirits. They are incredible navigational systems that inform us constantly, from our gut instincts to our hearts' deepest yearnings. But take a quick look around you and you won't see much acknowledgement of that truth. We are taught to ignore our gut instincts and be polite instead. We are taught to ignore physical hunger and work to be stick thin if we are women. We are rewarded for overworking, often at the expense of our health, thus raising our stress levels even more. We are taught to live from our heads, ignoring our bodies' wisdom.

And as we lose touch with our bodies, our healthy resilience suffers. "Speed kills" refers to more than highway statistics. The amount of complexity in our lives can be overwhelming. The speed of modern technology, combined with the sheer volume of information thrown at us in any given day, is enough to make anyone feel like they cannot slow down and breathe, if they want to keep up.

The good news is that, although changing slowly, the present state of body awareness in America is beginning to improve, as seen in the increasing numbers of people going for bodywork and attending yoga or movement classes. While there is this growing recognition of the value of the mind-body connection, there is also a growing awareness of the problems resulting from the alienation from our bodies—our disrupted body presence—letting us know that we still need to be *even more fully present in our bodies* and our lives. This is particularly so if we hope to be able to help others in a way that is more rewarding and less stressful.

Stress in the Healthcare and the Care-Giving World

As I teach in the healthcare world, I see the results of disrupted body presence exhibited in the exhaustion—and stress-related illnesses—of my students. The effect of burnout on bodyworkers, caregivers, and other healthcare professionals is well known and has serious effects on the individual, the family, and society.

If you have a burned-out healthcare provider with diminished therapeutic presence, important cues and signals can be missed and mistakes can be made. This is further aggravated by the mountains of paperwork now required in treatment, that leave little or no time for the wonderful nourishing parts of the job, by staff cuts that leave those still employed to do the jobs of two people, and by a lack of healthy resources for these support-givers.

More importantly, very few healthcare providers and caregivers are taught how to stop, tune in, and take care of *themselves* so they can more effectively take care of others, without burning out. In fact, the default stance that many in healthcare operate from is to give without any thought of themselves. Their satisfaction and their self-worth is measured by the results of their efforts on behalf of others, with self-care being seen as selfish or self-centered.

Another key factor is that caregivers and healthcare providers often suffer from the effects of ministering to the needs of those who are in pain, stressed out, grieving, and often anxious or scared. The provider, to some degree, often absorbs this state of tension and fear from the patient if they don't know how to have healthy boundaries.

One choice taught in some healthcare modalities is to distance oneself from a patient or client. This can work to a degree, but it effectively numbs the healthcare provider so that they lose the ability to take in the positive, life-giving aspects of their work. The care provided is then limited and the compassion is missing. These people become a mechanical healthcare delivery system rather than a conduit for deep, lasting healing and care where all parties can benefit. Burnout is then not far behind. The need for restorative steps is clear.

Mind-Body-Spirit Connection

In recent years a great deal has been discovered about the intimate interplay between mind, emotions, and body. We have clear evidence of how our *emotions* are intimately connected to *physical* distress and illness. Yet, for all the exciting new therapeutic approaches to working directly with the body in ways that restore health and awareness, the value of actual full body presence is still not well recognized.

The sensory awareness aspect of full body presence—the grounded connection with our own bodies and the world around us—can play a major role in the healing of physical symptoms and illnesses. It can assuage and ultimately transform fear, doubt, and alienation into a sense of trust and confidence in oneself and life as a whole. Thus, developing this awareness is also a powerful means of personal transformation. Furthermore, full body presence—the foundation of a strong therapeutic presence—is of vital importance both for caregivers and those receiving care.

Beyond that, full body presence leads us to a more solid connection with our innate spirit and energy. This *can* be the ever-present background against which we live our lives, not just the serendipitous, isolated minutes of connection and ecstasy that we may occasionally experience.

In many spiritual traditions on the earth today, heaven is synonymous with being fully connected to the Divine, to our spiritual source. Yet this visceral sense of connection, which is—or should be—a given, slips away from us as we are socialized to fit in to our hierarchical and compartmentalized culture.

Unfortunately, elements of our educational system, our cultural practices, even our religious doctrines, speak in terms of dominating our world and our environment, of controlling our bodily functions and our very thoughts, as if we are somehow separate from the rest of creation. Our emphasis on speed, instant gratification, outward appearances, staying competitive and retaining power without regard to the long-term outcome, leaves us little time for feeling and meeting our deeper physical, emotional and spiritual needs.

In this milieu, our deeper *felt* needs are relegated to a lesser status. With regard to large or small issues, the wisdom of the body and its signals are suspect and not to be trusted in our culture. We typically give our thoughts more weight than our more non-linear inner knowing. We put our trust in outside experts to figure out what to do in our lives, rather than taking external data and going inside ourselves, contacting our deeper wisdom, to know what is best for us. Lacking trust in our own internal awareness, we close down our sensory awareness, *creating a sense of separation from our world*, event by event, as we grow up.

Origins of Disrupted Body Presence

Our trust in our instincts and awareness can erode in many ways. Perhaps there was a time when you felt sick as a child, but you were told you were fine, so you began right then to doubt your own internal cues.

Perhaps there was a time when you were grief-stricken because a friend moved away, but you were told that your grief was not important, or shameful, or at the very least, unreasonable (you had plenty of other friends, right?). So you mistrusted your own feelings and began to lock away your grief whenever it arose in the future.

Or perhaps you had an uncle who gave you a creepy feeling when he hugged you at family reunions, but when you mentioned it to another adult, you were told to "quit being silly; how could you think such a thing about your uncle?" So you began to distrust your internal knowing that told you your boundaries were being violated in some way.

Or maybe you had a friend you *loved* with all your heart. But others made fun of you for loving so openly and whole-heartedly. Or perhaps you were rejected, so you began to close down how much love you let yourself feel or the level of inspiration for living that you allowed yourself to experience.

In each of these examples your body was telling you something important and those around you were trying to convince you that what you were sensing wasn't real or valid.

Trauma and Defense Responses

No matter where we grew up, we have all had to adapt in order to survive, to be accepted, to conform to the expectations of our families, our religious traditions, and our culture.

Depending on our innate temperament, and the level of repression to which we were subjected, we behave according to our own unique adaptations and defenses. Many of our idiosyncratic defense mechanisms may have originally served as brilliant survival tactics, particularly if we overcame traumatic events or circumstances. However, in most cases, these adaptations are now obsolete. They are impediments to our happiness. They add to our sense of separation, from our world and ourselves.

When traumatic events happen to us, the natural human tendencies are to respond to the stress by freezing, feeling numb, forgetting what to say, wanting to run, or fighting back to defend ourselves. Trauma can cause a temporary or long-term disruption of our full body presence. The focus is on survival and survival alone. Our nervous systems automatically go into a high state of arousal, which can lead to skewed perceptions and reduced energetic awareness that can affect us in detrimental ways.

An additional issue is that we often lose touch with our internal navigational systems and all that they have to offer us, in terms of *wisdom* and *safety*. When we are not fully present in our bodies due to past or present trauma, we have a disruption in our system that needs to be resolved.

Building Your Present Moment Awareness Skills

If at times you feel overwhelmed by your feelings, you'll find the audio *Explorations* will help you learn how to develop your body and energy field as a container that can hold and modulate the whole range of human emotions. Building and continually strengthening this container enables you to have feelings and learn from them, rather than having to constantly suppress them for fear of being overwhelmed or embarrassed by them. During times of stress or personal tragedy, this can be particularly important.

In my twenty five years of teaching this work, I have watched thousands of students not only understand, but also come to embody, the present moment awareness skills in this book. I've watched students move into the deeper resonance and connection to life that is our birthright as human beings. It is in this state of flow with our deepest spiritual knowing that we can feel the peace of being alive, fully in our bodies in each present moment.

LISTEN:
Your body is speaking to you.

Chapter 2

~

How I Learned to Trust
My Body's Signals

My awareness of the invisible energy dynamics that connect us all that I shared with you in the Introduction slowly continued to expand after that summer night's experience in Washington, D.C., when I was ten years old.

When I was 17, I received my first big lesson in how my body could act as a barometer capable of sensing these invisible energy dynamics—informing me of the rightness or wrongness of certain situations in my life. Many of us have had a gut sensation when something felt really off—a sense of danger. Had I then had the confidence to trust my body's signals as I do today, the following story would have played out very differently.

One Saturday night, deep in the warm summer of 1971, I was spending time with an old friend who, unbeknownst to me, was in withdrawal from a long stint of being awake on amphetamines. As we sat together in his car in the parking lot outside of a neighborhood pool party, having a normal friendly teenage conversation, I began to feel a strange but distinct uneasiness in my gut. It was not from the tone of his voice or the topic of discussion. The uneasiness continued for well over half an hour, and I continued to ignore it because it was unreasonable to feel uncomfortable around him. He was such a close friend, like an older brother to me. Besides it would have been impolite to say anything about it. The next thing I knew his hands were around my throat and he was strangling me. He was so strong that I passed out, quickly and completely. When I regained consciousness, I was trembling all over, my head pressed against the car door. He was plastered to the other side of the front seat, behind the wheel, obviously shocked and horrified at what he had done, apologizing profusely.

I, too, was in serious shock. Every cell in my body was screaming at me to get out of the car *now*. This time I listened. I managed to open the door and crawl across the parking lot to a friend's car where help was waiting. It took years of emotional healing and bodywork to melt the internal scars of betrayal and fear from that event. If I had paid attention to my gut and honored the message it was giving me, I could have avoided the whole situation.

Several years later, having regained the trust in my "gut knowing," I was able to avoid another potential disaster. I was on a date with a popular basketball player in college. We were sitting around at a party in someone's dorm room drinking and laughing. The music was loud and people were having a good time. Suddenly I noticed that other people were leaving. Soon, he and I would be the only ones left. My gut began to give me that odd alarm signal that I had experienced but not listened to earlier. This time I listened. I made an excuse about needing to go to the bathroom and left for good. I discovered later that he had date-raped several other women on campus. While I had learned the hard way initially, I *did* learn how to listen to my gut about danger.

What about the other body signals of this invisible world of energy dynamics? Next, I discovered what I needed to gain an understanding of breath and conscious movement, and bring that practice into my life.

Just before I left for college in the fall of 1971, I took my first yoga class. *I loved it.* Somehow I instinctively knew that the conscious awareness I was being taught about breath, movement, and slowing down might possibly bring me closer to being able to connect *intentionally* with the experiences I had previously undergone only serendipitously. As I faithfully practiced the yoga asanas and meditated each day, I began to notice a quieting in my system that I had never known before, as well as a growing ability to hear what my body was saying to me.

My last year of college brought me a firsthand experience of how my intention and full body presence could combine to create a powerful synergy. I was in a dance performance in which I was a tree. My entire role was to stand solidly, center stage. Another dancer, a young man probably 40 pounds heavier than me, had to climb up one side of me and down the other. I was chosen for the role because I was the only one who could stand that strongly and firmly.

I did this by taking my conscious awareness inside my body and feeling myself growing roots like a big oak tree, down into the stage floor, and on down into the earth. Once I was rooted, I was almost immovable. I could walk away when I wanted to, but I also could create such a strong connection to the ground under me that my presence was like a human oak tree.

Everyone else was amazed that I could hold the weight of my fellow dancer who was much larger than me, but to me this ability was simply an extension of what I had been playing with for several years. Later, I would learn that in the martial arts, and certain meditation practices, this same use of intention and body awareness was well known. And I was discovering all this on an adventure of my own; curiously exploring intention, energetic connection, and full body presence.

My Parents' Presence

My parents' attitude toward life and their own willingness to continue growing throughout their lives was a great example for me. The ways in which they were limited by their life experiences affected me as well.

For instance, my mom took me to my first yoga class, which was a pivotal part of my journey. She also has a gentle, quiet energy and a huge, warm heart. On the other hand, like many women in her generation, when I was growing up she didn't know how to have healthy boundaries—she let everyone walk all over her. She had a hard time asking for what she needed. And everyone else's needs came first. So, from my mother came a natural ability to be a warm-hearted presence, *and*, a huge question as to how I could be powerful *and* female.

My father was an incredible thinker and a powerful public speaker. I grew up wanting to be *just* like him. He had a presence that commanded attention, which gave me permission to do the same. The flip side was that his public presence exhausted him. What I discovered later on is that my father had ready access only to his mind and upper body which left him with a disrupted body presence, depleted and exhausted at the end of every Sunday service.

What my parents were unable to convey to me was an appreciation of my lower body and all that the lower body represents—gut instinct, sexuality, intense creativity, movement, and grounding. Although I had a loving family, as I grew into adulthood, I understood that both my parents had deep issues of shame around their sexuality. Both of them experienced childhood traumas, causing them to energetically withdraw from their lower halves, severely disrupting their ability to have a full body presence. My parents did not pass on the abuse they had received; however, their fear of lower body energy left a gaping hole in my understanding about what lower body presence feels like in a healthy person.

We were Baptists. As often is the case, my religion taught me to judge and control my body. Full-hearted singing and righteous (upper body) presence is what was exemplified. There was no energetic modeling for full body presence—the energetic awareness of upper body *and* legs, feet, and pelvis. And this is vital for being able to support a compassionate heart consistently throughout life, for being able to enjoy yourself and feel present in each moment.

Moving Beyond My Legacy

Yoga and meditation practice helped begin to bridge the gap left in me when I followed my parents' example. From these practices, I began to feel *more* present throughout my entire body. I am eternally grateful for what I learned there. Yet I ultimately realized the limits of these ancient systems. They were highly codified and rule-bound as to how one should experience the body. The underlying premise is that the breath, and the body it fills, are something to be brought under control.

I was still being told how to *control* my body rather than exploring its natural, unique exquisiteness.

In most religious and spiritual systems being practiced today, being connected to life, to God, to the Universal All, the Tao; ultimately means controlling and *leaving* your body, not fully inhabiting it. This didn't feel right to me. And, I was learning to trust my body and my gut feelings. So while I continued my daily yoga and meditation practices—growing my "energy muscles" and learning to focus—I instinctively kept searching for something more.

The birth of my first child catalyzed a journey to make my spiritual practice a more *practical* part of my life. My 17 years of having an hour a day dedicated to spiritual practice was done. I am sure many new parents can relate. I could no longer take time out to create the steady peacefulness that an hour of any legitimate spiritual practice can provide. I now needed a way to connect to healthy resources in the *midst* of my life instead.

The same year my daughter was born I began teaching CranioSacral therapy regularly and needed to find something that I could practice on a moment-to-moment basis to provide a strong, integrated presence as a teacher in the classroom. How could I bring full body presence to my life with all the challenges that parenthood and work brought?

It was at this point that the Five Principles of Full Body Presence (you will read about these in the next chapter) were first conceived. I began to distill the wisdom I had learned from the many teachers and spiritual practices I had the honor to receive. The wisdom from the lessons learned while bathed in the rich resonance of singing on that front pew as a child all the way to learning how to hear the whispers of wisdom from the rocks, trees, and animals that my indigenous teachers taught me.

I was clarifying the principles behind how to set a laser-like, focused intention and follow it, and then how to surrender to the all-encompassing flow of life energy available to all of us.

I was also learning how *trusting* in this flow opened more possibilities for my healing and growth, and how *feeling* life's energy in my own body and letting it *integrate* throughout my system, gave me more access to my gifts and my vitality. I also began to recognize how using my mind as an ally, rather than a critic, *expanded* my capabilities as a therapist, teacher, mother, and wife. Finally, learning to *choose* moment to moment those things that were most life giving, for me, helped me move from the exhaustion and overwhelm of infant care and work to enjoying my life and family again.

I needed to be able to discern a healthy direction in my life on a moment's notice. I needed to understand how the navigational system of my body operated optimally and what to do when it was awry. I needed to have clear, simple questions to ask myself that could guide my day. These Five Principles did that for me. I have been refining them over the last twenty five years. So what you see in the next chapter is a "tried and true" set of guidelines that work hand in hand with the *Explorations*.

So what follows here is a practical, step-by-step process that comes from the fruit of all my searching, designed to help all of us be more fully present in our bodies and our lives. In all the years that I have been peeling away layers and learning to move into the truth of who I am, I have been deeply challenged and deeply rewarded. Walking this path feeds and amplifies my creativity. I have developed confidence in what I am doing because I have learned to act from the core of who I am.

I have witnessed this same process of evolution in my students over the past 20 years. They consistently tell me how this work catalyzed them into making their dreams a reality, helped them make peace with things in their lives that they were struggling with, or allowed them to deal with a personal tragedy without shutting down.

As I removed the layers of fear,
doubt, resistance, anger, and denial,
my life's purpose became increasingly clear.
Now let's bring clarity to your life.

Chapter 3

∼

The Five Principles of

Full Body Presence

Like signposts on the path of life, the Five Principles of Full Body Presence are used to help you create optimal, healthy living. They name important concepts about how the invisible energy dynamics of the universe operate. As you explore the deeper meanings of these principles, you may notice that the framework they present is familiar. The reason is that these principles, in one form or another, underlie the core teachings within the spiritual doctrines of most major religions. By understanding and then using these principles in your everyday experiences, you are not only embracing skills that can heal your life and bring you greater joy, you are gaining access to greater support for deepening your own spiritual practices, whatever they happen to be.

The illustration of the Five Principles of Full Body Presence *(see page 26)* honors the symbol of the circle—a core structure found everywhere in nature. Everything comes full circle as through life, death, and rebirth in the seasons on our planet.

We all live within the circle of the earth and its magnetic field and the sea of energy that we are swimming in all the time. From the circular shape that we see in the structure of our cells out to the stars in the heavens above us, we are all interconnected.

As seen in the Medicine Wheel of indigenous cultures, there is the recognition that no one part of the circle dominates, or is more important, than any other element. It is about balance and the understanding that everything has its place and is important in some way.

In that same vein, these Five Principles are interconnected in what they have to teach us. If the principle of *Trusting* is a challenge for you, you may find that to trust more fully you need to include the *Expanding* principle so as to see your world in a clearer more accurate way. With a more expanded lens on the world, you can then work with the principle of *Choosing* more healthy resources for yourself, which helps you have better outcomes in your day. This in turn helps you with *Trusting* and be open to new possibilities. All the while, your full body presence is increasing.

The Five Principles provide guidelines for working with that invisible sea of energy in your life at a physical, emotional, mental, and spiritual level. Each of these is of equal importance to your wellbeing. Alone, or in combination, each principle will show up in your life at times of stress or healing, demanding your attention. The correct starting point or entry door into your own circle of healing or transformation may shift for you in each circumstance of your life.

Sometimes you may find that you are working primarily with one of them for a while—for instance, the principle of

Feeling the Presence of Life Energy in Your Body. You may recognize that you have trouble feeling much of anything internally. This makes decision-making difficult as you constantly second-guess. So you begin to practice the skills taught here, and one day, when a stressful situation pops up, you realize that you have the principle of *Feeling.* Where before you would have struggled to know how you felt or what you wanted, you discover now that you can easily drop inside and know exactly what to do and where you need to go.

This may then lead you to the principle of *Choosing Nourishing Resources Moment to Moment* as you realize that you now can choose more wisely for yourself because your inner compass, your navigational system is more fully operational. You can now weave the fabric of your life with healthy resources that leave you feeling more energized and steady.

Usually, what you need will call to you as you read this chapter. Recognizing which principles resonate with you and then addressing what they are pointing out to you will enable you to increase your full body presence—mastery of your life, your health, and your creative process. Let's get started.

The Five Principles of Full Body Presence

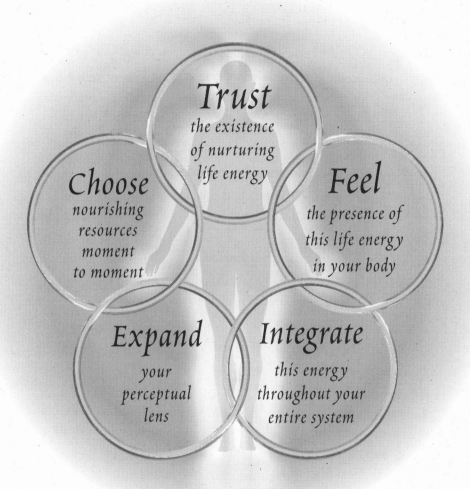

Trust
the existence of nurturing life energy

Choose
nourishing resources moment to moment

Feel
the presence of this life energy in your body

Expand
your perceptual lens

Integrate
this energy throughout your entire system

Principle 1
TRUST the Existence of Nurturing Life Energy

Trusting that there is an unlimited source of nourishing, life-giving energy in the Universe allows you to recognize that you are loved, and supported throughout your life, and allows you to live from trust rather than from fear.

Quantum physics has shown us that, at a molecular level, we are all connected, swimming together in this sea of energy. The core of many spiritual traditions refers to this unity by different names—the Universal All, God, the One, the Tao, the Collective. But its essence is the same. This source is timeless and endless. It is unconditional in its offering, in its connection to us. Though we may not feel connected in certain moments to this sea of energy, we all have access. It supplies all of us with an ever-abundant healthy resource.

I trust my ability to connect to healthy resources.

This field of energy is a constant support for leading healthy, vital lives. As you develop confidence in your relationship to this boundless source of energy, it is easier to trust and to handle what life brings you.

This principle of *trusting* is what energetically underlies the work of a broad spectrum of successful people who have written prolifically about self-help and living your best life.

When Norman Vincent Peale, in his primer, *The Power of Positive Thinking*, says to "*always* picture 'success,' no matter how badly things seem to be going at the moment," he is referencing the fact that when one *trusts* and, thus, continually pictures support, even when it looks otherwise, the support has a much higher probability of being recognized when it shows up.

When Martin Seligman, the father of positive psychology and "learned optimism", describes how the pessimism and the depression that accompany negative thoughts can be overcome, he clearly delineates how the skills he teaches rest on re-establishing trust. The trust that opens the doors to possibilities not seen previously.

An attitude of trust and trustworthiness affects all aspects of my life.

Stephen M.R. Covey, in his book, *The Speed of Trust*, has brought forward a whole new facet to this principle of *trusting* as he points out that the advantage in today's business world is in how fast a product or service can be gotten to market. He clearly delineates how *trust* increases the efficiency of organizations and *low trust* impedes the whole process by creating hidden agendas, interpersonal conflict, win-lose thinking, and defensive communications. He states that:

> Trust is like the aquifer—the huge water pool under the earth—that feeds all of the subsurface wells. In business and in life, these wells are often called innovation, complementary teams, collaboration, empowerment . . . these wells themselves feed the rivers and streams of human interaction, business commerce and deal making.

This principle speaks to what happens energetically when an *attitude* of *trust* is established and put into *action* in our lives. When we learn to trust that support is there for us, and lean into that trust, it leads us right to the doorway of many new possibilities. This is much more powerful than simply visualizing a positive outcome and tenaciously trying to hold onto it.

One of my colleagues tells the story of her basketball-playing eleven year-old son. His coach was working with the team to set up positive visions of themselves and their playing abilities. Unfortunately, her son had set his vision to be the perfect player, never missing a shot and being the star of the team. Although it was an admirable goal to reach for, every time he missed a shot it crushed him and crippled his playing as his entire vision collapsed around him.

I trust that I am supported by my world.

Between games my colleague quietly suggested to her son that he choose a vision of himself playing his best, with his team all supporting each other, doing their best possible teamwork that day. He liked that vision better as it opened possibilities without absolutes. With that, not only did his attitude improve dramatically, so did his playing!

The capacity to be open to discovery is an important first step in any healing, growing, or manifesting process. Being open requires trust and that is what this principle acknowledges.

Many people can agree with this principle in theory, but find it hard to trust in moments of uncertainty or depletion. Or they become overwhelmed when it *appears* that there is no support available. Yet it is in those very times when life gets challenging that we most need to remember this principle. We have all had painful, scary experiences at some point in our lives that may have felt overwhelming. Our world or certain aspects of it, suddenly feel dangerous and unfriendly, or we decide *we* are somehow at fault.

When either of those decisions becomes a default stance in our lives, often unconsciously, we can find ourselves, particularly in times of stress or uncertainty, struggling to find healthy resources and solutions. This is because our basic underlying default stance keeps cutting off the trust that there *is* a nourishing, nurturing source of energy we can tap into. And when that trust is gone, it disrupts our ability to have full body presence.

You probably know someone who is surrounded by love or is supported in some way they *cannot* see or feel because they are constantly on guard, waiting for the other shoe to drop. In all likelihood, they have developed strategies that don't work very well, to tightly control their world in a misguided effort to keep it safe. From their disrupted body presence, they are unable to take in the support that is available to them. They may often walk right by it, with no recognition that it is there.

In what areas of my life do I trust in myself and my abilities?

How might you tell if this principle is calling *you* to pay attention to it? You might know because under stress or in personally upsetting situations you have thoughts, or resort to actions or words, that reflect fear or anxiety that serve to block you to possibilities and healthy resources that might otherwise assist you.

This might take the form of blaming those around you rather than taking appropriate responsibility for yourself and your actions that would move you in a more positive, helpful

When I am in a state of trusting, I am most aware of feeling it here in my body.

direction. It might look like you are taking *too much* responsibility and wrongly blaming yourself. It might manifest as you withdrawing, contracting, or freezing in place so that you don't have to experience fully what you are afraid is about to happen. It might surface with your attacking whoever is closest to you in an attempt to fend off the real or imagined enemy.

Clearly, this principle of *Trusting the Existence of Nurturing Life Energy* affects decision-making. Decisions based on trust differ significantly in quality and results from decisions based on fear. Trust creates an openness to discovery, which in turn unlocks the door to more of life's possibilities. It also opens us to the energy of life so that we are connected to what we need.

One of my colleagues reports that when she is in a tight spot and cannot actually feel trusting of this support, she *acts as if* she is trusting, or imagines herself having a conversation with someone she knows does trust, and then diligently directs herself to take actions that open up those new possibilities. She finds that the trust and support inevitably follow.

So the key is to train yourself to *remember* that this unconditional source of energy *does* exist, and to pause and connect with it in *whatever way you can in each moment*. Then the possibilities and options become clear and more accessible, and you are able to stop the cycle of negative thinking. You are able to begin to trust.

When you reach the part in this book where you listen to *Exploration III*, you will be taken deeply into a process of healing and rewiring your nervous system to be able to accept a new, more pleasurable, healthy reality. When this principle is practiced regularly, relaxation and openness to new possibilities can happen for all of us.

Principle 2

FEEL the Presence of Life Energy in Your Body

Feeling your internal connection to this life energy as a natural state of being opens your awareness to discover a sense of belonging, reclaim your inner wisdom, and experience vitality and joy.

The ability to feel a sense of connection to the larger universal energy honors the innate intelligence of your body as an internal compass. As you deepen this connection, you can learn to navigate by your own internal compass rather than the world's expectations or by relying solely on input from others.

Principle 1—Trust, points out that we are all connected, all the time, to the universal source that makes up the field of energy we live in. Principle 2—Feel, goes on to state that from the moment we are born, we are meant to have a deep, *felt sense* of this connection to ourselves and to the world around us.

When that experience is present, there may be a sense of tingling, warmth, elation, open-heartedness, calmness,

My sense of spiritual connection and oneness with life shows up here in my body.

quietness, joy, knowing, flow, creative thought, powerful-ease, nourishing-fullness, bliss. As Candace Pert says in *Molecules of Emotion*, "We're hardwired for bliss." We operate best from that state of connection, active, conscious participants in the flow of life. We experience a visceral sense of belonging—in our own bodies! This state of feeling fully alive is our birthright.

There are many ways to *consciously* connect with this ever-present source of life energy. You may already have ways that increase your energetic awareness, such as an experience of feeling peaceful in a favorite outdoor place, walking on the beach, hiking in the woods, sitting on a massive rock, feeling a wind brush your body, reveling in the warm sun on your face, or being rocked gently by ocean waves.

While this connection to the vast sea of energy is available through your experiences in nature, it can also be *felt* through calming breath, prayer, and meditation of all kinds. It can be felt through the resonance of singing or chanting or however *you feel* renewed from this universal, loving energy. In the audio *Exploration II*, we use imagery to connect with the rich field of the earth—grounding, feeling firmly rooted, receiving whatever would most nurture and nourish us in that moment. With each repetition of this *Exploration*, we strengthen and reaffirm our ability to *feel* that connection—deepening our energetic awareness and refining our ability to navigate through our world from *inside* our bodies.

With this innate sense of connection to life comes a natural sense of vitality and joy. I saw this most clearly in both of my children when they were younger. When my son was two, I remember being amazed by his spontaneous, unimpeded flow of energy, curiosity, and aliveness. The delight and openness with which he drank in all life had to offer, and the generosity in this outpouring of love in return, was a pleasure to be around. Looking back now I would say he had exquisitely tuned energetic awareness that allowed him to live in his full body presence most of the time.

One afternoon at the circus, when the elephants burst through the curtains in all their glory and glittery costumes, I thought my son would burst with joy. His eyes lit up; he shrieked and laughed and clapped and called to them, drinking them in with all of his senses, as their smell filled the tent, as the lights glittered off of them, and they strolled and turned and showed him all of their magnificence. He was enthralled. Full body presence at its best!

When I am feeling most energized, I feel it here in my body.

But, at another moment, when someone would reject him or life wasn't giving him what he needed, his grief could be all-encompassing as well. He was connected *to it all* and the waves just rolled right through. Over the course of a day, he could go through a broad spectrum of feelings: pleasure and pain, ecstasy and disappointment, anger and sweet tenderness. It amazed me! He lived in the present moment, in the flow of life. When I watched him, I recognized the capacity for connection to life that we *all* have, however buried or repressed it might be.

Because of the life experiences, which over time have caused us to dampen or even fully shut down our own connection to the fullness of life, we may have to relearn how to access it. We experience that connection through having energetic awareness of the internal landscape of our body, and listening carefully to its inner wisdom.

Our innate cellular intelligence informs us constantly, like an inner compass of deep knowing. It is a hunch that something is off in a relationship or a sense of rightness about a project that makes no sense logically yet makes our heart sing. It might be a direction we somehow know we need to take or it might be someone we instinctively know that we need to avoid at all costs.

This deep wisdom comes from all parts of us. Sometimes we can feel an ache in our heart or a tightening in our gut. At other moments we might experience it as a whisper of instruction about a person or situation that is confusing. It might come as a memory of an event from long ago that reminds us of something we need to learn from in this moment. The body's inner compass of wisdom is always there. We do not always know what it is saying or how to hear it.

I recognize and honor my gut feelings, as well as my heart's desires, and include both in my life choices.

It's not the norm in Western culture to listen to our insides, to take the time to slow down and focus on internal awareness, and to make decisions based on our deep inner-knowing. Instead, we tend to be driven to move forward and accomplish everything that is expected of us, regardless of what we truly want (if we even know what that is) or how we are feeling *inside*. If anyone asks, we smile and say we're doing fine, while continuing to run on automatic pilot. We focus on *doing* rather than *being*.

Disrupted Energy Flow

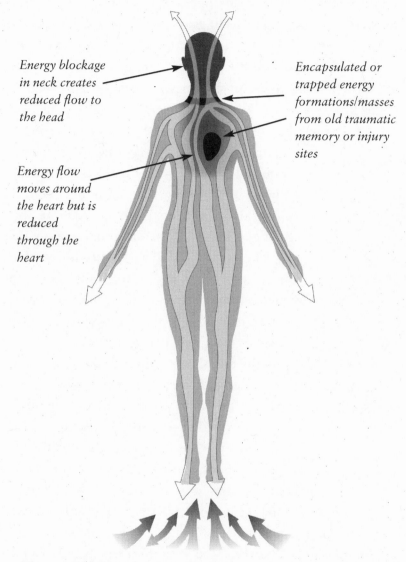

Energy blockage in neck creates reduced flow to the head

Encapsulated or trapped energy formations/masses from old traumatic memory or injury sites

Energy flow moves around the heart but is reduced through the heart

In this example, the energy flow through the heart and throat are disrupted due to past traumas or injuries. This is a common human experience—having either large or small areas, really obvious or very subtle places, that don't feel as connected to the rest of us.

35

When the experience of feeling connected to yourself—your internal landscape—is disrupted or absent, then fear, hopelessness, despair, or feelings of being overwhelmed often arise. You may feel isolated or have a sense of not belonging anywhere. Physically these feelings can manifest as intense pain, a dull background ache, an emptiness, a sense of clenching, or feeling run down. These are some of the sensations of a disrupted body presence.

I recognize when I feel less connected, and I feel it here in my body.

It's important to *acknowledge* that you're feeling separate and to notice what that feels like in your body. By first *having* that awareness of the disruption in your system, you are more able to make a new decision and move in the direction of establishing a connection to what nurtures you. It's also important to understand that the experience of *feeling* separate, though it seems very real, is actually *only a perception*. You are never actually disconnected from life.

Remember, we exist within this sea of energy all the time, whether we are conscious of it or not, whether we choose to acknowledge it or not. When you are able to feel this healthy life force within your body, you not only regain your sense of belonging. You tap a vast reservoir of intuitive knowledge and guidance as you experience the vitality of a healthier, more joyful life.

Another issue that comes up with this principle is looking at what can impede or support our ability to feel our insides. *Nurturing physical touch encourages a healthy internal sense of self—* increasing our energetic awareness—while a lack of nurturing touch causes a sense of numbness and pain. It's been my clinical experience that there is a *huge lack* of nurturing touch in our world today. This results in a *reduced ability to sense our internal landscapes* and feel steady and grounded. Touch has become largely sexualized and exploitative in our culture. When the touching we have in our lives is not safe and nurturing, the automatic response is to pull away from it. This greatly contributes to the sense of separation that is currently so prevalent.

Lack of loving touch also affects our ability to grow, mature, and flourish as a species. We know from recent infant and child attachment research that a child who feels a secure physical and emotional connection to at least one parent develops the neural pathways for resilience, and those that miss out on those nurturing physical and emotional connections have a much harder time consoling themselves, calming their anxieties, and tolerating high levels of pleasure and excitement.

I accept and enjoy nurturing, healthy touch.

Nurturing, non-invasive touch is a major component in developing the healthy resilience that we all require in today's world; yet, many of us, if we grew up in the average American household, are operating from a touch deficit. One that we may not even be aware of. We simply *do not know* the deep nourishment that can be felt from enough consistent, caring touch and holding.

As Ashley Montague so clearly pointed out in his landmark book, *Touching: The Human Significance of the Skin*, he shows from worldwide research, that it is a biological *need*, an *imperative* to the healthy development of all infants, their nervous systems, their intelligence, that they be held and bonded with as much as each baby needs and wants.

Think about what you probably grew up with in terms of nurturing touch. Many of us simply have no context by which to understand what I am saying here, no frame of reference for what we have never experienced. If this applies to you, you may find that you don't reach for, feel comfortable with, or easily accept, the healthy, sensual, pleasurable connections of being alive that healing touch can provide. People who were held and touched *enough* on that nourishing physical level as infants and children have a better chance of having an ongoing, expanded capacity to experience pleasure in life and to reach more easily for healthy resources.

The good news is that we can heal this. Through creating channels for nurturing touch in our present day lives, we can increase the neural pathways of healthy resilience that we missed early on developmentally.

Again, the latest research in brain function and neural plasticity shows that the brain and nervous system change continuously throughout life, in response to new input. These changes in our nervous systems are powerfully influenced by our current, ongoing experiences.

These influences can take many forms. There might be a nurturing partner or friend who hugs you frequently. It could be getting regular nurturing bodywork such as: massage, CranioSacral, or any of the other healing touch systems that *really listen* to your body and respond to it in a nurturing way. It might be a pet that snuggles and cuddles with you. It could even be something as simple as sleeping on sheets that feel wonderful to your skin, like flannel or satin. Or it might be taking baths or showers that give your skin a good feeling of warmth or coolness that it craves. In other words, there are many ways in which we can create for ourselves the healthy pleasures of touch that grow our nervous systems.

Every nurturing, pleasurable sensation that we can let in, everything we learn, every healthy intimate contact we make, causes millions of neurons to fire together, forming new physical interconnections within the body. These neural networks are what comprises healthy resilience. Healthy resilience allows us to *feel* a sense of connection to our world that is reliable and consistent.

Within this framework, our energetic awareness grows, and we can navigate wisely from within our bodies. We then have new possibilities for greater vitality and joy every day of our lives. Our full body presence can become the foundation we live from in each present moment of awareness.

Principle 3

INTEGRATE this Energy Throughout Your Entire System

Integrating a felt sense of this nurturing energy throughout your entire body helps you establish a full personal container with strong, flexible, healthy boundaries.

By consciously choosing to open *all* your channels to receive nurturing energy, you gain access to more and more parts of yourself. You will also find yourself in the present moment more easily and more often. You create a strong container from which to process and heal your own pain, and you gain the capacity to hold a powerful healing presence for someone else.

You learn intimately where you stop and the rest of the world begins. This is what is meant when we talk about having healthy boundaries. It is easier to maintain healthy boundaries when you have a nourishing flow of energy throughout your body—your container. Your skin, and the energy field that flows through and around it, is a boundary to be respected by everyone.

I can sense when someone crosses my boundaries and say 'no' when something does not feel right to me.

When your container is full of nourishing energy, you have a clearer sense of yourself. You can choose to connect more deeply with the world around you. You have a clear choice about what to do when you encounter someone else's negative energy—be it a client, family member, or a stranger.

With healthy boundaries enclosing vital, nourishing energy, you also have a much greater capacity to hold a healing space, a strong therapeutic presence, for another person without depleting yourself. In fact, the more you practice this principle, the more likely you are to come out of such interchanges with *more* energy rather than less. The full body presence that is the signature of a full container enables you to hold this space for another person effortlessly. Your therapeutic presence provides a calm, centered quality of being that feels healing, steady, and safe to those around you.

Principle 1—Trust, invokes the power of *trusting* our connection to this sea of energy that we live in. In doing so we open more fully, in a conscious way, to new possibilities and discoveries. Principle 2—Feel, invokes the power of *feeling* that life force, that energy, viscerally within our bodies. In doing so, we open to the possibility of more vitality and joy in our everyday lives.

Present Moment
Sensory Awareness

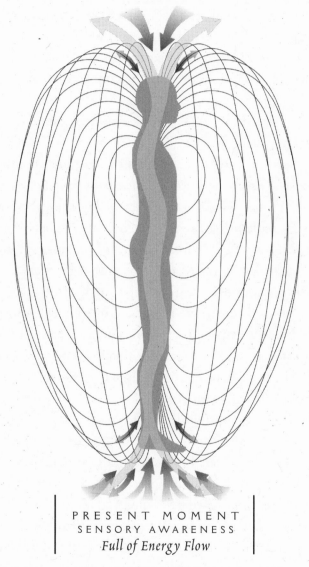

PRESENT MOMENT
SENSORY AWARENESS
Full of Energy Flow

Full body presence enables our navigational system to operate optimally, with clearer communication between all the parts of ourselves.

This third principle invokes the power of *integrating*, of having this unconditional energy source available throughout your entire body—your bones, your muscles, your belly, your feet and legs—allowing the very cells of your body to soak up nurturing, nourishing energy as best you can.

In this process, you are creating a stronger flow of energy in your body. From this core level of connection you can allow your energy field to grow—to widen and expand—creating a strong, integrated presence. You have more of yourself available to enjoy your life.

Principle 3—Integrate, teaches that we are *meant* to have *every part of ourselves in communication with every other part,* and that everything works *best* when our energy supply is continually replenished, so that we operate *in the flow* of life.

However, most of us don't have *all* of ourselves in this ideal communication because of traumas, either physical accidents or emotional traumas. Traumas that lock us out of parts of ourselves or cause us to get frozen in time making those parts inaccessible to us in the present moment. Stress, illness, and exhaustion also contribute to the disrupted body presence that is the outcome. There is no judgment here—just the simple recognition that we function best when all parts of our navigational systems are fully operational.

I see our future, as a species, hinging on whether we can learn to live fully in our bodies, rather than rejecting parts of ourselves as sinful, bad, or dangerous. This is not easy to do; in our culture, we can easily be derailed and intimidated. But if we can learn to listen to our inner wisdom, ultimately, we are able to make of our bodies a stronger physical container, from which our souls can create whatever we came here to create.

Invoking our full body presence calls our life force, our

spirit, our soul, home to us, allowing it to fully inhabit and inspire us, rather than leaving our bodies in order to make a connection to the Divine. There is an innate integrity that comes into play, beyond external rules and morality, when we are making decisions and creating in our world from a more fully integrated place.

Think about it. When you have more energetic awareness in the present moment and are listening to all parts of yourself—such as your gut, your heart, your mind, your feet and your legs—whatever decision you make is bound to be wiser than if only one part of you is dominating the process. You would not try to drive a car with one part of the engine not working. When that happens it starts to pull the rest of the engine into breakdown, like driving with not enough oil or without all the cylinders firing. Yet, we routinely grow up being told not to feel or live in certain parts of ourselves. Then we wonder why we have blind spots or difficulties when we encounter events in life that require the wisdom of the part of our bodies that we don't live in.

Each part of us, literally every cell, has an innate intelligence. It is there to inform us, in every moment, of what it needs and what it can give to the rest of the body for its health and wellbeing. *Listen, your body is speaking to you.*

When you develop a strong physical container that is flowing with energy, it is easier to be in this present moment of life and feel the joy that is here now. You also become strong enough to hold and heal past or hidden traumas without becoming re-traumatized or emotionally overwhelmed. Your *very presence* is healing.

A full container is also important to give you a cushion of resilience in order to prevent burnout from excessive life stressors. When you feel more full and in the flow of what nourishes you most, you have healthy boundaries. With healthy

Sensing Disrupted Energy

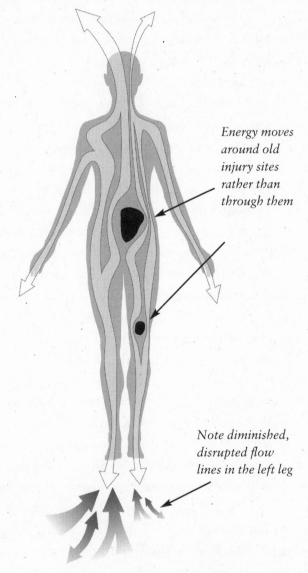

Energy moves around old injury sites rather than through them

Note diminished, disrupted flow lines in the left leg

Growing energetic awareness leads to a heightened ability to sense areas of flow and connection as well as areas of disruption in your own internal landscape.

boundaries, you are more easily able to protect and support yourself, because you are sure that your needs are being met while still having your heart open to the world around you.

As your integration expands and deepens, you will have a more intimate sense of your own internal road map. You will sense where it is that you have a greater flow of energy. You will also sense where it is that you have less— areas where you may feel blocked or locked out of as you seek to generate greater aliveness. You will identify your own unique energy habits. This deeper connection is essential to the entire healing process.

Does the container of my being feel good and full of life?

The key to this principle of integration boils down to recognizing and exploring all your emotions, thoughts, and beliefs with curiosity, and having the courage to let every part of your internal landscape inform you of *its* wisdom. This means that if you have been afraid to explore what's in your heart or how much tenderness you feel there, you can build the trust and courage to go into your heart more fully—rather than defending, rejecting, or protecting yourself from your heart's desires and requests.

This principle of integration also means being willing to feel your belly and your pelvis, those foundational areas of power and support in the body. When there is a clear connection and flow of energy from the pelvis and the belly to the heart, the heart is supported and held in a more consistently powerful way. You have more energy to create and follow through on your heartfelt desires. This might mean, however, first having the courage to reclaim your pelvis and to stand in your power.

And speaking of standing, when you can fully inhabit your pelvis, feet, and legs, and feel connection with the earth, you can walk in your world connected to healthy resources, with your inner knowing guiding your way.

Think of your body as your unique, personal navigational system for inner knowledge and guidance about how to operate optimally in the world. The more fully you can inhabit all aspects of yourself—physical, emotional, mental, and spiritual—the more access you have to your inner wisdom. The more access you have to that quiet voice of deep knowing that guides you so beautifully when you can hear it. When you are in your navigational system fully, you know intimately where you are, who you are, and what you need to thrive. You know how to connect when that is desirable and how to hold your boundary when that is appropriate and necessary. And, the fullness of your being enables you to be a strong presence in your life and the lives of those around you, with grace and ease.

Principle 4
EXPAND Your Perceptual Lens

Expanding your perceptual lens enables you to see clearly,
release expectations and limiting beliefs,
and open fully to life.

Our ability to open to life also depends on the width and breadth of our perceptual lens. As the lens of our eye defines our visual field, we use the metaphor of a perceptual lens here for how we perceive our world—not just visually, but through our sensations, our thoughts and beliefs, our memories, and our dreams. Whenever the lens of the eye is narrowed or distorted, our visual perception is often skewed and limited. In the same way whenever our beliefs, memories, or expectations are narrowing our perceptual lens, our life experience is limited.

Our perceptual lens can be invisible—outside of our conscious awareness. It often forms the background context from which we live our lives. Our perceptual lens is based on our judgments—our interpretation of events—filtered through our beliefs, expectations, emotions, bodily sensations, and feelings. Because this lens is frequently narrowed in some way, our ability to realize our hopes and dreams, to live an authentic life, true to ourselves, is often severely compromised.

When we open to new possibilities or take in new experiences, our perceptual lens naturally expands. It can expand or narrow multiple times in any given day, depending on how we interpret events and interactions that come our way.

Is my perceptual lens wide enough to recognize my gifts and talents?

The linear mind, and its dominance in our culture, make this principle particularly important. We are prevented from fully experiencing life when we live from our heads and discount our body sensations. As we begin to move in a healing direction, one of the first stumbling blocks most of us run into is the narrowness of *how* we perceive ourselves and the world around us. We are hamstrung by our limiting beliefs, having internalized the messages delivered so powerfully by our culture.

So we began in Principle 1 by *trusting* the existence of a

nurturing life force. We took it a step further in Principle 2 by *feeling* this life force within us, and in Principle 3 by *integrating* it throughout our system for optimal living with deep connection and healthy boundaries.

Do I tend to think others are better or smarter than I am, even though it might not be true?

Now Principle 4 invokes the power of *expanding* your perceptual lens so that you can open your mind—allowing your thoughts to become your ally, rather than your enemy. I often think of an overactive, dominating mind as a captor, holding your conscious awareness prisoner. Many forms of meditation and contemplative prayer have guidelines that revolve around getting the mental chatter—the Internal Judge—out of the way, thus enabling the quiet, inner voice of your deeper, spiritual wisdom to be heard.

There is more to life than we can imagine if we open ourselves up to the possibilities without incurring the immediate judgment of the mind. Having said that, let's admit that *all of us compare and judge.*

Do I tend to hold the conviction that I am better or smarter than everyone else?

At one moment, you may believe that someone in your life is smarter, more evolved or clearer than you and that you'll never measure up. Moments later, you may decide that someone else in your vicinity is self-indulgent and talks too much, or that you can't stand the shirt he is wearing. At moments you may feel grandiose and superior to others. At other moments you may feel as if you are stupid and you'll never "get it." These are just the natural gyrations of a narrowed, defensive perceptual lens.

Awareness Being Pulled Into Past Experiences

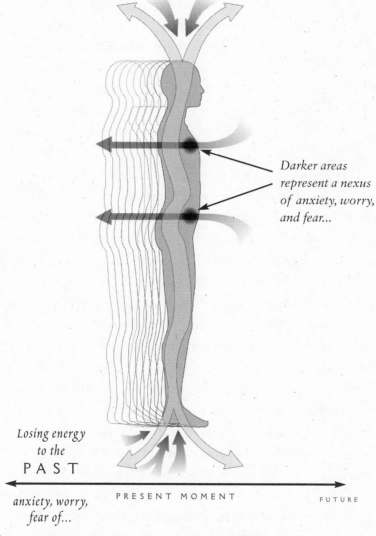

Darker areas represent a nexus of anxiety, worry, and fear...

Losing energy to the
P A S T

anxiety, worry, fear of...

PRESENT MOMENT

FUTURE

When conscious or unconscious awareness is pulled into past experiences, traumas and events, the result is that the perceptual lens narrows and this prevents you from being fully present in the moment.

49

Typically, when you're looking through a narrowed perceptual lens, it's because some aspect of your past is coloring your present moment experience, and thus your outlook on your future. You are looking through your own filters that prevent you from fully seeing yourself, and the world as it is, in this present moment. So how can you move beyond this? How can you open your mind, recognize your judgments and limiting beliefs for what they are, and invoke this principle of expanding your perceptual lens?

What judgment or limiting belief comes to mind right now?

Building on all the other principles we have talked about so far—*feel* inside your body; *trust* the flow of energy moving through you—*filling* and *integrating* the container of your being. Once these three are in place, you will begin to notice more acutely when your lens has narrowed—when you're caught in a limiting belief. Notice what it *feels* like in your body when your energy field tightens down around thoughts of hopelessness, numbness, or despair? Notice *the feeling* when you live with grandiose thoughts that require you to maintain a mask or persona that is not really you? These feelings are indicative of a disrupted body presence that is the signature of a narrowed perceptual lens.

Tune into the tightness or the charge you feel when you've passed judgment on someone or something, and you are sure with a vengeance that you are right and the other person is wrong. Or, tune into the sensation in the pit of your stomach when you feel like you are not good enough in some way. See if you can *simply notice* these feelings and sensations with as little judgment as possible. And, in that noticing while holding them in a more neutral, compassionate way, there is the opportunity to choose to expand your lens.

Awareness Being Pulled Into Future Possibilities

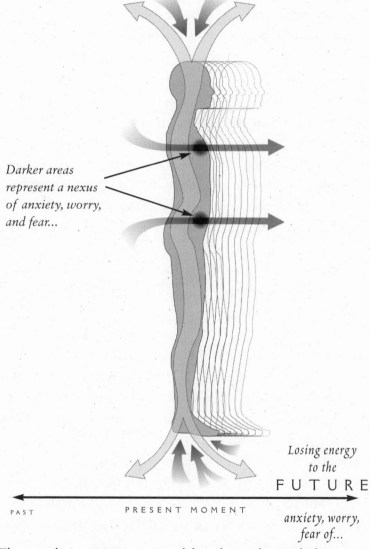

Darker areas represent a nexus of anxiety, worry, and fear...

Losing energy to the
FUTURE

PAST

PRESENT MOMENT

anxiety, worry, fear of...

When caught in anxiety, worry and fear about what might happen in the future, you are pulled out of the present moment, which is energetically draining and also narrows your perceptual lens.

51

So let's look at the steps of this process a little more closely.

First: Become energetically aware of the charge, the tightening, in your internal landscape that happens around seeing the world in a certain limiting way, *without drowning in it or blindly believing it.*

Second: Recognizing that *in this present moment* this perception is not necessarily true, questions the validity of the perception and begins to shake loose its hold on you. After all, you really *don't* know if it's true or not. The challenge is to try to stay as neutral as you can and *not* give credibility to the old voices in your head. The voices that are reminding you of all the times you thought you weren't good enough or that you failed.

Third: Open to the *possibility* that there are other ways to perceive yourself and that you *can* have a new, more expanded, easier experience in your body.

Last: Explore *exactly what* it would feel like in your body, to whatever degree is possible in this moment, if you *were* good enough and you *could* imagine succeeding—letting yourself just imagine what that would feel like on an *emotional* and *sensory level* within yourself. As your body lets go and lets in the new experience, you have just expanded your lens in a very powerful and grounded way. You have moved beyond simply *thinking* about a new way of being and brought it all the way into the *bodily experience*, as well. The healing can move completely through your system—mind, body, emotions, and spirit.

An anonymous poet offers good advice on beliefs:

If I continue to believe as I have always believed,
I will continue to act as I have always acted.
If I continue to act as I have always acted,
I will continue to get what I have always gotten.

See Chapter 7, *Exploration III: Healing the Internal Resistance to Life,* for examples of how to work with and transform resistance and the tunnel vision of our perceptual lens in many areas of our lives. Knowing how to break that cycle of living from our limiting beliefs and becoming open to new sensation possibilities is what this principle is all about. This truth permeates every area of our lives. When we can practice it regularly, it will set us free.

Principle 5

CHOOSE Nourishing Resources Moment to Moment

Choosing moment to moment to connect to healthy resources requires commitment, courage, and kindness, and provides you with a steady foundation and a deep sense of inner peace.

Learning to consistently tap into healthy resources and listen to your body takes ongoing practice and needs to be embedded in the fabric of your life, into your daily routines and activities.

It is important to remember to nourish and nurture yourself, no matter what the situation. The airlines are correct. It is important to put *your own* oxygen mask on *before* assisting those in need around you. This may require a change in what you pay attention to. If most of your daily attention goes *outside* of yourself to pleasing and accommodating those around you, making sure you fit in, even when it is to your detriment, you will need to change this orientation. But, by balancing your attention *inside* and *outside* of yourself, you can gain a new ability to choose healthy resources moment to moment. In fact, you may find that holding a therapeutic presence for someone else is actually a pleasurable and easy process once you are listening more to your own insides and nourishing yourself sufficiently.

Sometimes you may need to begin by choosing something small, but honestly do-able in your life as it stands now. After my father died, my mom made sure that she shared one meal a day with someone else in order to stay in contact with the nurturing people in her world. This simple choice helped her stay connected in a way that was easy for her at that time. Now, nine years later, her network of friends and activities is rich and wide. But it all began with one easy step taken each day.

What healthy, nurturing resources can help me wake up and begin each day with more energy?

Each person is unique and what is nourishing for you may not be nourishing for someone else. Ultimately, only you can know and choose what is most nourishing for you in any given moment. I am reminded of my mom and dad who found going to an inspiring film to be a wonderful way to relax and refill their energy stores. The issue was that they had *entirely* different ideas about what constituted an *inspiring* film. So they would go to the multiplex cinema together and each would attend their own different *inspiring* film, meeting afterwards for tea and sharing. This is an excellent example of having a healthy boundary—nourishing oneself and having it work well for everyone else as well.

Throughout this book and with the audio *Explorations*, you are exploring various ways to access a multitude of healthy resources that you can choose from, depending on your temperament, your mood, and your needs on that particular day. These resources can enable you to heal yourself and hold a healing space for others. You will also explore the ways in which you lose your sense of connection to life-giving resources, often under stress, so that you can learn to reconnect and stay connected much more of the time.

What healthy resources can nurture me during my working day?

At the heart of this principle is the fact that it is not enough to know *how* to connect to your nourishing resources. It is paramount that you give yourself permission to make healthy choices on a regular basis so that the habit grows strong enough to carry you when things get stressful. This is why regular—perhaps daily—practice of *Exploration II* is so important; it is a primary source for building and maintaining that nourishing energy flow in your container—your body. It is then easier to discern what other resources are healthiest and perhaps most pleasurable for you in any given moment. To keep your navigational system fully operational, maintain a solid baseline of energy so you can make better decisions in your life.

It also takes courage to walk your own healthy path. Often in our culture, our media bombards us with ways to fill the emptiness, to numb pain, and a sense of disconnection with a variety of addictions such as: excessive shopping, drugs, alcohol, compulsive sex, too much television, endless computer internet surfing. The list goes on. The strategy of addictions is avoidance—fear of facing a part of yourself and whatever pain or anxiety might come up in the process. Although addictive substances and actions may ease the pain temporarily, ultimately they are life taking—sucking the energy out of the healthy, creative, nourishing areas of our lives.

What healthy resources help me settle down and get a good night's sleep?

Having the presence of mind to choose to refill in a healthy manner, so that you can meet and dissolve the pain in life-enhancing ways, means you are generating new energy habits that will lead to a lifetime of wellness on many levels. Whenever you start feeling doubtful, fearful, or empty, let those feelings be a signal to you. Let them remind you to feel your feet, to connect to the rich energy of the earth, to take a slow, deep breath, to say a prayer, to take a walk, or to do whatever nurtures and fills you up in a healthy way.

Choosing healthy resources moment to moment is our birthright and always an option. There are all kinds of healthy resources to choose from: an experience of feeling peaceful resting back in your favorite chair, reveling in the warm sun at the beach, hiking in the mountains, feeling a breeze blow through your hair, floating in a quiet pool, slowing and deepening your breath, meditating, having a quiet cup of tea while your child is at preschool, or calling a good friend to catch up.

One of the most important resources we can avail ourselves of is the nurturing physical touch I described in Principle 2-Feel. One of my favorite choices for healing and rejuvenating is giving myself permission to get good bodywork. Nurturing touch of all kinds fills me up wonderfully. My system needs differing kinds of bodywork, depending on where I am in that moment. A good massage for slowing down and refilling is great.

I can learn from my mistakes and make healthier choices.

The most valuable healing bodywork for me has been CranioSacral therapy, because it enabled me to heal years of chronic pain and feel more of my body's internal landscape in a pleasurable way. I still return to it regularly to stay clear and healthy in a world full of stress and deadlines. When I forget to schedule regular bodywork sessions or other nurturing experiences, I find myself slipping into working harder than I need to and feeling less energized, with less present moment awareness.

The other most valuable healthy resource in my life has been movement. Whether it is a good daily walk or a retreat with days of internally inspired movement, I come away feeling juicy and more alive.

Brainstorm your own particular list of things that nurture you in a healthy way. One day it might be to take a long soak in an Epsom salts bath. Another day it might be a long run followed by a sports massage. Another day it might be getting to spend time with good friends, sharing activities that you all enjoy. It could be listening to inspirational music that feeds your soul. Keep adding to the list and exploring new events and activities. Be a detective on your own behalf. Be constantly ferreting out what nurtures you in a *healthy, pleasurable* way.

And, please don't criticize yourself if you forget that it is your highest natural state of being to be connected and full of life. Be *kind to yourself*, as you would be to a good friend. Find the place within that feels disconnected and hold it with unconditional love. Do this as often as necessary until the sense of separation is healed. In some cases, to simply remember the sensations of connection and filling are enough. Remember your intention to heal yourself, to reclaim your energy and your dreams. Remember the practices that fill you up in a healthy way and do one of them, even if only briefly. This is a moment-by-moment process that will become more natural as you practice it. Eventually, it will be as natural to you as breathing. A sense of steadiness and inner peace will become a part of your daily existence. Then you will know that you have entered into communion with life itself.

*Make a choice now to notice these principles
when you are in a situation that challenges you—
your new awareness can change both your response
and the outcome.*

Chapter 4

∼

The Three Explorations
The Secrets of This Practice

At the heart of *Full Body Presence* are the three *Explorations* on the accompanying audio download or CD. These three *Explorations*, which you are encouraged to listen to repeatedly throughout your work with this book, are the main tools used to reconnect you with your body and the energy of the universe: energy that is always available to you.

In my 20 years of working with these *Explorations*, I have seen many people use them effectively, and they have facilitated huge transformations. I've seen other people struggle with certain elements and walk away before they got what they needed, because they didn't fully understand how the process works.

This chapter will give you the information that is critical for you to understand how to get the most out of the *Explorations*. By reading this chapter before you listen to the audio, you will fully understand the concept of *Explorations* and the basic guidelines for maximizing your experience.

The critical distinction between the *Explorations* in this

book and more traditional guided imagery techniques is that these are non-directive. They are meant, as their name implies, as a vehicle for you to *explore* your own sensations and feelings, to expand your own inner knowledge and awareness, without being told exactly what you should expect and how to interpret what you find. These *Explorations* are designed to build and refine your sensitivity to your internal landscape and to help you discern and integrate the connections between your inner world and the world around you.

This is vital, because experiencing life from *inside* your body is the key to fully inhabiting your world. Your body is an incredible navigational system. Almost anyone can take in what's going on around them at a logical, mental level. However, if that is the limit of your conscious level of comprehension, you are missing a great deal. Deepening your sensory experience of who you are inside, at your core, gives you a strong, solid reference point for living your life.

The three *Explorations* are the foundation for this process. Each has a specific purpose, though they are often used in tandem.

Exploration I, Opening Awareness: Where Am I in This Moment?, is designed to help you assess your current awareness of your relationship with your body. You'll be working experientially, listening for subtle cues and sensations to which you might not normally pay attention. You will be establishing a baseline reading of where you are most present in your body and where you are not as present. Many of my students and clients return periodically to this *Exploration* in order to note changes as life brings them a new day. It can serve as your barometer of energy, and of progress.

Exploration II, Nourishing and Replenishing the Container of Your Being: Grounding and Filling, teaches the all-important concept of understanding and developing your body as a container—a safe, strong vehicle—for your energy and spirit. This is accomplished through a process of staying connected to the rich field of the earth, as well as the other healthy resources described in the introduction, and continually filling and replenishing yourself. *Exploration II* is the exercise you may use most often, perhaps on a daily basis, to maintain the integrity, strength, and resilience of presence in your body.

Exploration III, Healing the Internal Resistance to Life, has the goal of helping you deal with the inevitable blocks that come up as you begin to reclaim and energize your whole body. This is the exercise you can use whenever obstacles present themselves— fear, alienation, confusion, conflict, detachment, negativity, lack of sensation, agitation, disconnection, feeling overwhelmed, physical pain, or illness—the issues that inevitably surface in our daily lives as we strive to more fully inhabit our bodies.

As you explore specific issues with regard to intimate relationships, family dynamics and friendship, work and money, limiting beliefs and personal growth, you can use *Exploration III*, in conjunction with *Explorations I and II*, to help remove those obstacles to healing.

Exploration Guidelines

A separate chapter is devoted to introducing and fully explaining each of the three individual *Explorations*. Each chapter describes the purpose and process of the *Exploration*, explains the philosophy behind it, and discusses its relationship to the Five Principles discussed in Chapter 3. The full text of the *Explorations,* as recorded on the accompanying audio, can be found in Appendix A at the end of the book.

All of the *Explorations* are designed to be experienced in a relaxed manner. Our body's internal landscape, as well as the sea of energy around us all, is rich with information and intelligence just waiting to be contacted. The following guidelines apply to all three *Explorations*. They will assist you in making this contact with your inner world more easily and help you to hear more accurately what is being conveyed to you from deep within or from without.

Atmosphere and Environment

There are many ways to engage this process. If you are already familiar with sitting in contemplative prayer, an embodied meditative practice, or journaling, please use what you already know. Add my suggestions where needed. Any practice where you filter out the chatter in the mind first and then listen to the quiet voice within is going to be a good place to start.

In terms of your physical environment, I find these *Explorations* are best done in a quiet environment, seated in a comfortable chair with good back support, your feet planted easily and fully on the floor. If your feet don't quite reach the floor, put them on a nice, firm pillow.

If you choose to do the *Explorations* lying down, bend your knees so that the bottoms of your feet are in contact with the ground. This is not an ideal situation because so many of us naturally fall asleep when we get horizontal, but it will work in a pinch.

Always feel free to gently move or re-adjust yourself in order to remain comfortable as the *Exploration* unfolds. The point is to be comfortable, relaxed, and, at the same time, awake and aware.

You will find it easiest to travel in your body's internal landscape if you close your eyes so that the majority of your focus turns inward. If you have a tendency to fall asleep when you close your eyes, you can allow them to remain slightly open with a soft focus on something in front of you that does not pull your attention. The point is to allow your attention to go inward as though you could turn your eyes, and the rest of your senses, inside yourself.

Who is Driving My Bus?

Our inner worlds are complex, composed of many different parts of ourselves, some long forgotten or never before heard from. There are ways in which our upbringing and life experiences have taught us to deal competently with life's complexity, and other ways in which our experiences have paralyzed us. To try to exercise some control over what parts of me are calling the shots at any given time, I use the metaphor of myself as a bus. All the parts of myself are the riders on my bus. My standard question to myself, when I am feeling down, or my inner critic is railing on me, is "*Who is driving my bus right now?*" When the more integrated, vital parts of me are driving my bus, I am aware of what is going on inside me, and what is affecting me outside the container of my skin.

If I am *not* aware of what is affecting me, a part of me that I may not have consciously chosen (say, my inner critic, my anxious self, or a younger, previously traumatized part) can easily hijack the bus and take it in a direction that is not life enhancing. I may find myself thinking, "I cannot do this, I am a hopeless failure," or, "I am bad—there must be something wrong with me." Or, if a grandiose part has hijacked my bus, I may find myself blaming others in order to feel good enough about myself.

These parts of ourselves may have served as necessary defenses at some other point in our lives; however, you can rest assured that they are not presently helping you to realize your dreams and potential. When you are able to become aware of and manage these assertive, wayward voices in working with the *Explorations*, you will be better able to maintain mastery in your life.

So if you find yourself stuck, or if judgments come up in any of the *Explorations* in this book, ask yourself, "*Who is driving my bus right now?*" Following that question, notice what pops into your awareness, without editing or judging. It, too, can inform you.

Once you have identified the critic, or the life-draining meddler, firmly but gently *remove* it from the driver's seat of your bus, and send it elsewhere. My personal tactic is to mentally escort it to the back row of my bus and keep it there. If it somehow returns to the driver's seat at some point later in the process, I again, gently but firmly, usher it to the back of the bus. This is a lighthearted but surprisingly effective way to keep the thoughts, that could derail the *Exploration,* at bay. Know that it is likely that you may have to repeatedly escort these troublemakers to the back of the bus. As time goes on and you work with these *Explorations*, they will lose power over you. We'll talk more about why this occurs later and offer some effective strategies to meet and disable them.

Put Your Curiosity in the Driver's Seat

The key to overriding sabotaging inner voices is to invite your curiosity on board. Invite your innate interest in your aliveness to join you in your *Explorations*. Allow your journey to be playful, not a forced march. Allow your openness to discovery to lead the way. Adopt an open-hearted, non-judgmental attitude, *as best you can in that moment*. This ability will be different each time you enter into the *Explorations*. You want to discern what your internal landscape feels like to begin with—with as much openness and as little editorializing as possible. If you notice your judging mind creeping back in as you go along, simply recognize it. Then intentionally get it out of the driver's seat of your awareness. Let a quiet, open curiosity take over again.

No matter who is trying to take control, allow *only* the part of you that is open to discovery to take the driver's seat of your bus. You can recognize this aspect of yourself because it won't be second-guessing everything you think or do. When it is 'driving your bus', you'll feel inquisitive and fascinated with life and your internal landscape. Leading with your curiosity, your openness to discovery, allows you to have a *direct experience* of your inner and outer world.

By direct experience I mean an experience that is not colored by interpretation. Direct experience means feeling sensations without immediate mental associations that put the experience in a box or categorize it. It is human nature to judge an experience and immediately categorize it. If you can catch

65

the moment quickly enough to allow yourself a short time of *feeling a sensation in a new way*, without interpretation, before the prior associations get attached to it, then you have a chance to experience your world with fresh eyes.

Fresh eyes give you a wider, more expansive experience. They are indicative of an expanded perceptual lens. Fresh eyes give you access to the present moment. So, whenever you are beginning one of these *Explorations*, remember to consciously ask your curiosity, your openness to discovery, to join you and drive your bus. Expand your perceptual lens as you go.

Your Goal is to Be Here Now

The goal-oriented perfectionist in us has to make an extra effort to shift focus from a goal line out in front of us somewhere to cultivating our curiosity about internal sensations, *moment to moment*. When we are focused on a goal, or expectation, the act of judging whether we've reached it or not separates us from the actual experience in the present moment. It slows down or halts the process of feeling sensation as our minds kicks in and jumps to interpretations of what this or that sensation might mean and how close we are to the goal.

This is, by definition, an *Exploration*. The point is to simply notice what you feel. Accept that whatever that is, it is okay. *Simply allow yourself to feel what you feel.* This means noticing sensations like *warmth, coolness, a sense of dryness, dampness, wetness or feeling slippery, an area of dense-heaviness, a spot that feels solid-steady, an area that feels light and spacious or one that feels empty, the impression of a color or texture, a hum or pulsation, a soreness or sharpness, a numb place, the sensation of being relaxed, anxious, or excited.*

Full Energy Flow

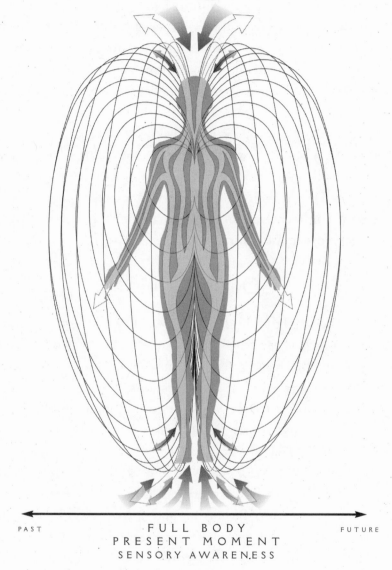

PAST   **FULL BODY**   FUTURE
PRESENT MOMENT
SENSORY AWARENESS

When you are connected to healthy resources, and there are fewer disruptions in your system, then the energy flow can move effortlessly through you. This exploration will feel different every time you practice it.

Also, know that *however much input you are experiencing*—sensations, colors, textures, intuitive hits—is just what it needs to be. Even if it is only a subtle whisper of feeling, like the touch of a butterfly wing, that's okay. Your ability to tune into internal sensation will expand and become more acute as you use these *Explorations* and learn to read the signals of your internal landscape.

Some people struggle initially to connect with internal sensations at all. But, when they stop and compare how they feel over all after they get done, they notice that they feel different. They may not be sure yet what changed, but it gives them the confidence to continue practicing, knowing that they will feel more in the future.

Question Cues

As you listen to the audio *Explorations*, I'll be asking you a series of questions. You can work with the questions or you can let my voice drop to the background of your conscious awareness, and let your curiosity ask your own questions.

As you listen to my voice or follow your own line of questioning, just gently *follow your awareness* to that place you've just asked about and see what arises: what the sensation is, what color seems to appear, the texture of that place inside of you. No interpretation, no story—just the feeling, the sensation. Be curious and open, always keeping in mind that this is an *Exploration*, not a test with right or wrong answers. Simply notice what you find; what it means will come later.

If you find yourself spacing out or your mind wanders away, simply bring yourself back to the *Exploration* as soon as you notice it. Sometimes this means bringing yourself back over and over throughout the entire process. Don't let it be a problem. Just return your focus to your internal landscape wherever you left off when your mind wandered away. Return to being curious about how you feel on the inside.

Honor Your Own Natural Process

This is *your* exploration. You get to do it in a manner that works for you. If you are highly sensitive, you may need to allow small amounts of sensation at a time, titrating your sensory input, so that you feel comfortable with it. In other words, if you *allow yourself to take it at your own pace*, you can grow your system into being able to handle more input at some future time. But if you try to rush it—trying to get to some self-imposed goal—your system will often simply close down or stop integrating what you are doing. If at any time during the *Exploration* you feel uncomfortable or disoriented, simply open your eyes and re-orient yourself, resting until you feel ready to go on again. Again, *this is not a forced march*. Do this at your own pace, in a way that works for you.

After Using the Explorations

Each time you have worked with an *Exploration*, document your experience somehow.

You may want to use journaling, drawing, or painting to record you experience. If you are journaling, write down as much of your stream of consciousness of the experience as you can remember. Don't worry about spelling or punctuation—just let it flow out.

Giving texture and color to your experience by drawing or painting your internal landscape can be equally valuable. Again, just let it flow out onto the paper. One of my students drew a mandala every day for a year, to reflect her experiences during her inner *Explorations*. What emerged was a colorful, beautiful record of her growth and transformation across that year.

Another option is to share your experience with another person or speak it into a recording device of some kind. One caution: If you are sharing your experience with someone, be sure they are just *witnessing* and not trying to interpret your experience as you report it.

Any of these activities immediately following an *Exploration* will help the whole system to integrate the experience: right brain to left brain, color and texture, sound and scent, any sensation or meaning from the deep unspoken level. It has been demonstrated that journaling your inner experiences can accelerate the healing process. So, use any or all of these tools, as often as time allows. They will add a whole new dimension to your life, often even opening the door to your creativity.

Bring your openness to discovery—
your curiosity—to the next page.

Chapter 5

~

Exploration I
Opening Awareness:

Where Am I
In This Moment?

"Being willing to listen to our bodies is the first step in the journey home to ourselves."

SUZANNE SCURLOCK-DURANA

M any of us these days live busy lives. And those who are not physically busy often find their current peace of mind crowded out by past regrets and future worries. No one has taught them how to take a moment to check inside as a reference point for their lives. They have not cultivated the habit of stopping in the midst of their hustle and bustle to take a few deep breaths; to get quiet and listen to their inner voice, that place inside them that can give them feedback on their feelings, their desires, their energy at that moment.

In short, they don't have a clue as to how to be *in* the present moment, rather than rushing through it. Unaware of their internal landscape, they just push on, taking care of what needs to be done, ignoring the wisdom of their bodies, the feelings and concerns that are clamoring to be heard. In fact, some people don't want to know what's going on inside. They keep busy. They fill every minute, aware on some level that if they slowed down and let themselves feel their inner turmoil, they would be overwhelmed. And then they might not be able to function—to work, to take care of the kids, to stay in the relationship or job they suspect is self-destructive. They do not want to face the long-held dreams that are escaping them with every passing day.

Exploration I could be called the "Check-In" exercise. Its purpose is to give you a framework for stopping and finding out who you are, what you are feeling, and what you want in this present moment. It is designed to help you assess your *current* relationship with your internal landscape. You'll be working experientially—listening for subtle cues and sensations you might not pay attention to normally.

You'll be taking a baseline reading on your current presence level—noticing where you are feeling most present in your body and where you are not. As you know by now, being in the present moment is everything—and this *Exploration* can help you move from where you are now to a deeper, more fully embodied presence, in your inner and outer worlds. Your present moment awareness will deepen with the *Explorations* that follow, but this one is the entrance gate. Without it we are left *thinking* about being present, but not actually *feeling* it.

Carol Re-Discovers the Wisdom in Her Body

A long-time student of mine recently lost her husband quite suddenly to a heart attack. In speaking with Carol throughout the first few months after his death, her words to me were,

"Thank you for this work—I hate to think where I would be without the skills to listen to what my body is saying to me, moment by moment."

"The first month was waves of grief, on top of funeral details, plus all the family expectations heaped on me. I began to have serious heart palpitations. My anxiety level was sky high. My own internal awareness was minimal at that point. I was busy taking care of everyone else. So I stopped, tuned in, and began to move back in a healthy direction based on what I was feeling inside. I got my heart checked out medically. When all the tests came back clear, it dawned on me what was happening. The night of John's death, when I woke up and realized that he was breathing his last breath beside me, I gasped in horror and froze. I have been unconsciously 'holding my breath' to some degree, ever since. When I checked inside, I realized my diaphragm was clamped down tightly and the tension in my chest was triggering my palpitations."

By using her internal awareness skills she was able to accurately assess her health situation and take the steps she needed. As she moved through her life from that point forward, she checked in with herself frequently. In doing so she made important changes. She slowed down the pace of her life and picked up the rest of her self-care habits again. She knew she needed to do whatever it took to start breathing deeply and fully again. She went in for a massage, got some emotional counseling, and talked more things out with friends. As she made her way through this time, she described how her body slowly, day by day, became her friend again— her inner compass for when she needed to stop, to rest, to let herself grieve, to go for bodywork, to take care of herself. She began to listen to her body as a vital ally rather than something to be controlled in order to meet other people's expectations.

Her words to me as we closed our last conversation were, "I know I can do this now. I have the skills I need. My ability to slow down, tune in, and listen really pulled me through. I feel like I have passed a final exam. I would never have asked for this magnitude of a loss to learn this about myself but now, having done it, I am amazed and grateful."

Carol's experience is a wonderful reminder that often we have the information we need to heal waiting inside to be discovered, when we can slow down and tune in.

Exploration I may be used periodically to check in and assess how you are doing, what you are feeling, how you are responding to a particular issue or process. Over time, it will become a barometer of your level of presence with yourself.

Before you listen to this first audio *Exploration*, I want to briefly review the keys to unlocking this process.

- Turn your focus inward
- Invite your curiosity to lead the way
- Adopt an open-hearted, nonjudgmental attitude
- Give yourself permission to explore
- Go at your own pace, one that feels comfortable for you
- Allow yourself to simply feel what you feel
- If your mind wanders, gently bring it back
- And, enjoy!

Now that we have set the stage, listen to Exploration I *and then return to this page.*

After listening to *Exploration I*, know that it is always helpful to augment your evaluation with writing in your journal, drawing, moving, or any other expressive way of capturing your experience. The following suggested journal questions may stimulate your thoughts and awareness. Feel free to use them if you find them helpful.

Journal Questions

1. What did you notice that was familiar to you in your internal landscape?
2. What surprised you?
3. If you can, describe any sensations, colors, textures, vibration levels, densities, and shapes that showed up during this experience.
4. What were your dominant thoughts and feelings as you began this check-in?
5. Was there a place in your body where any of those thoughts or feelings were anchored?
6. What places felt frozen or inaccessible, and what thoughts, if any, came up there?
7. What places felt ease or lightness, and what thoughts, if any, came up there?

8. How did any of that shift or change across the course of the *Exploration*?
9. What stayed the same throughout the *Exploration*?
10. Did any part of your body's internal landscape inform you of anything that you need to take action on in your life?
11. Was anything a puzzle that you want to percolate on?
12. How soon would your internal landscape like you to check in again?

∽

Allow yourself to simply feel what you feel.
Stop, tune in, and listen.

Chapter 6

~

Exploration II
Nourishing and Replenishing
the Container of Your Being:
Grounding and Filling

*"Cultivate the root. The leaves and branches will
take care of themselves."*

CONFUCIUS

S tress, tension, overwork, anxiety, worry. These are
hallmarks of everyday life for many of us. Sometimes it
seems like we're all driving in the fast lane. These steady
pressures accumulate and, over time, take a stealthy, life-
sapping toll on our energies and our ability to cope with our
responsibilities. More importantly, our ability to take pleasure
in our lives is affected. It can get to the point where our bodies
are so depleted that our minds get muddled. We forget things,
or lose things, or find it exhausting to do what we need to do.
We are tired and susceptible to illness. Our bodies seem to be
letting us down. We have lost our resilience, our ability to
bounce back, and enjoy life's experiences.

The body is perfectly capable of healing itself, capable of restoring our energy, but it isn't simply a matter of diet, pills, or taking time off. The body needs to heal from the inside, from the core. That is the gift of *Exploration II*. It takes us on a journey home to ourselves. It helps us replenish and refill our life force so that we can heal.

Sarah's Health Returns

Daily chronic pain had been a part of Sarah's life ever since her car accident three years before she came to see me. As I treated her old injuries with CranioSacral therapy, her system responded beautifully, but my treatments were not as effective as I knew they could be. She was not holding the therapeutic gains made in our sessions.

As we worked together further, she realized that she was not completely healing from her injuries because she was so busy that she never had any down time. And when she did take time out, she had no idea how to deeply rest and receive what her body needed. She was always in gear, ready to go. She had been that way all her life. Carrying the whole load for her family, and doing a great job of it, was the way she had always done things.

She worked with *Exploration II* to learn how to replenish herself. She was amazed at how tired she felt the first time she tuned into her system. This passed as she gave herself permission to slow down and receive the nourishing energy that her system needed so badly. Next, we brainstormed how she could create resting time for herself every day. She committed to practicing with *Exploration II* every morning and building her day's schedule around what her body needed that day.

Initially, it was extremely difficult for her to break the habit of doing it all for her family and not getting the rest she needed in the process. But as the weeks passed, and her lifelong self-discipline became her ally, she gave herself one small self-care item every day. She continued with the bodywork and did *Exploration II* every morning. Then she discovered that when she did it in the evenings, it helped her sleep. Within several months, her pain completely disappeared as the treatments held. She had more energy for her life and her family. When we last spoke, she told me that she still used *Exploration II* at bedtime, because it helped her relax and get a better night's sleep. This gave her more energy for the next day.

Her experience reminds us that sometimes healing is a matter of changing how we see ourselves and opening to the simple, yet profound, process of connecting to an unconditional, healthy resource, and allowing it to fill and nourish us.

I call this process, of replenishing and strengthening the body, 'grounding and filling'. As it's name implies, this guided *Exploration* will help you learn how to plant yourself, grounding, more firmly on the earth and open to absorb its nourishing energy so that it courses through your body, filling, from your feet to your head and from your core to the boundaries of your skin. Over time this heals and fortifies areas of pain, numbness, weakness, or emotional distress.

Not only is this process vital for healing and vitality, it is also extremely valuable in times of stress, panic, and even danger. This *Exploration* helps us become a strong, steady presence, more able to bring all of ourselves and our resources to bear in any given situation.

Lisa in Danger

Several months after taking my basic course, Lisa awakened to a man with a gun standing over her bed where she and her boyfriend had been asleep. Her report of what happened follows.

"He was jumpy and skittish, and I was initially terrified that he was going to impulsively strike out and shoot us. He tied us together in the bed and left us in the dark, telling us he would be back for us. My boyfriend froze, but I remembered your words and began to ground myself and use the calming breath you taught us. When the robber came back into the room a few minutes later, I talked to him calmly and clearly, asking him what he was looking for and giving him directions to find what he wanted. As I continued to ground myself and we talked he became less agitated. I calmly asked him not to hurt us, told him that we would give him what he needed, and he quieted down even further as I continued to ground and fill—all the while lying tied up in the bed! Several times he left us and returned. Eventually he left the house, leaving us unharmed. Given his initial agitation and instability, I honestly don't know if I would be alive today if I hadn't had that training. Staying grounded and steady probably saved us, as I negotiated with the robber calmly and clearly until he left. I wouldn't ever want that to happen again, but I do now know that I can stay steady, grounded and present, even under the direst of circumstances. I think this is vital for dealing with the uncertainty and trauma so present in these times."

Exploration II is the foundation process for healing yourself. It is a satisfying and rejuvenating process, giving you a steadiness in your body that no one can take from you. I encourage you to take the time out for yourself to do it as often as possible, ideally every day, to strengthen and nourish your body's internal landscape. Do this so that you receive what you need for your own healing, so that you can take care of your own needs and responsibilities. Ultimately, able to be fully present to the needs of others you care for without feeling overburdened or burned out. In fact, once you have built up your inner resources and established strong boundaries to contain the energy, you will have plenty left over for yourself or those you love.

Reminders:
- Turn your focus inward
- Invite your curiosity to lead the way
- Adopt an open-hearted, nonjudgmental attitude
- Give yourself permission to explore
- Go at your own pace, one that feels comfortable for you
- Allow yourself to simply feel what you feel
- If your mind wanders, gently bring it back
- And, enjoy!

Now that we have set the stage, listen to Exploration II *and then return to this page.*

Now that you have listened to *Exploration II* it is helpful to augment your evaluation with writing in your journal, drawing, moving, or any other expressive way of capturing your experience. The following suggested journal questions may stimulate your thoughts and awareness. Feel free to use them if you find them helpful.

∽

Journal Questions

1. What did you notice that was familiar to you in your internal landscape?
2. What surprised you?
3. If you can, describe any sensations, colors, textures, vibration levels, densities, and shapes that showed up during your experience.
4. What were your dominant thoughts and feelings as you began this check-in?
5. Was there a place in your body where any of those thoughts or feelings were anchored?
6. How did any of that shift or change across the course of the *Exploration*?
7. What stayed the same throughout the *Exploration*?
8. Did any part of your internal landscape inform you of anything that you need to take action on in your life?
9. Was anything a puzzle that you want to percolate on?

∽

When you are grounded and full,
you are strong and steady.

Chapter 7

~

Exploration III

Healing the Internal Resistance to Life

"People say that what we are all seeking is a meaning for life. I don't think that's what we are really seeking. I think that what we're seeking is an experience of being alive, so that our life experiences on the purely physical plane will have resonances within our own inner most being and reality, so that we can actually feel the rapture of being alive."

JOSEPH CAMPBELL

fter working with *Explorations I and II*, you are probably feeling stronger and more confident, more resilient and capable of facing life's demands and your own desires. You are probably more aware of the problems and deficits in your life, and you may be less willing to simply tolerate them. But, what can you do? The thought of making changes or demands—requesting more time with your partner, setting healthy boundaries with your child, asking for a deserved raise, learning a new language—make you nervous and queasy or may even paralyze you.

One of the things that we have to recognize, whenever we are consciously waking up or feeling more energized, is the part of us that is afraid to take that next step, the step that will bring us into more aliveness. There's a word for that feeling: resistance. Resistance surfaces when we want to do something beyond our comfort zone—outside of our known world. Resistance is different than having a healthy boundary—and saying "no"—when something truly is not right for us. Resistance is that part of us that is afraid to move forward—the part that says "never", "I can't" or "I shouldn't". Many of our unhealthy, unproductive behaviors originated as a means of self-protection. We learned to withhold our opinions, to do what we were told, to follow an acceptable career path, to marry an acceptable partner, to keep our anger under wraps, or to use our anger as a shield, to dress in a way that wouldn't draw attention—the list goes on and on.

Until we start to wake up and explore what's inside us, we hardly notice that we are living by rules that are stifling us. Ironically, it is often those very rules that are keeping us from getting what we want in our lives. Once they served us well, or at least allowed us to get by under the circumstances in which we were brought up. They may now be outdated or even self-destructive.

Even so, we often cringe at the thought of the possible consequences of change, convinced that we will suffer the loss of those we love and what is familiar. It's the normal human reaction, and it can exert a tight hold on us. And yet, for all our internal resistance, the more we explore our internal landscape, the more we crave that sense of full aliveness. *Moving through your resistance can give you a breakthrough to experience full body presence.*

This chapter is about facing and overcoming resistance within our lives. It discusses the many forms resistance can take. Then we'll move right into *Exploration III*, the powerful, internal, alchemical process for working with all forms of resistance. Chapter 8 shares anecdotes and case histories to illustrate situations in which resistance arises, and offers guidelines for custom-tailoring the *Explorations* to address the places where resistance arises in different areas of your own life.

Masquerade

Resistance has many faces. Most of us are well aware of some of the ways in which resistance shows up—areas in our lives where we are afraid to move forward or are habitually gripped by some emotion that stops us, such as fear of public speaking or a fear of heights.

Other aspects of our resistance are more subtle and less conscious, such as resistance to receiving love or praise, or living fully in our power.

Our resistance often takes the form of somatic symptoms. These may include chronic physical distress that we have carried around, which may manifest as tight muscles or painfully restricted motion in different parts of the body. They are the parts of us that are rigid or frozen—numb or in pain. Of course, not all pain or physical blocks manifest as a 'face of resistance', but they often do.

One of my clients, Robert, came in complaining of tight muscles and painful restricted motion in his neck and shoulders, which were stooped as though he were carrying the proverbial 'weight of the world'. Robert was having a great deal of difficulty in his job. He had been receiving negative feedback that undermined his confidence in himself and his capabilities. The criticism from his boss launched him into childhood memories of his critical father and his powerlessness to stand up to him. The paralysis in his current job and the pain in his neck were directly connected to his resistance to acknowledging his fear that he wasn't good enough for the job—so similar to the feeling he had as a child who would never be good enough for his father.

After having worked with all three Explorations over a period of several weeks, Robert came to realize that his neck and back pain was directly connected to his early fears that had completely overwhelmed and paralyzed him as a child; he recognized that his current physical symptoms were actually his body's resistance to feeling that fear again. The pain subsided and the normal motion in his neck returned as he was able to meet that fear and resolve it. He was freeing himself up to take action at work, to speak up and rebut the negative feedback, and resolve the issues he was facing there.

It's All Your Fault

Underneath the more conscious faces of resistance is a deeper kind—one we all have difficulty recognizing and owning up to. This is the resistance we blindly project out onto the world around us—blaming someone else, or circumstances beyond our control, for the distress we feel inside. Even though our projection is unconscious, its effects in our lives—and the lives of those around us—can be quite powerful and destructive.

Sometimes it takes me *weeks* just to identify this kind of resistance as mine so I can take responsibility for it, face it, and work with it. The more honestly I explore my internal landscape, the quicker this awareness can rise to my consciousness.

For example, when I am having a heated disagreement with my husband, and I am fully convinced of how 'right' I am, I eventually may realize that it is my own stuff being projected out onto to him. Then I know I need to look deeper to see how I am *really* feeling underneath all that self-righteousness.

If you are married or partnered with someone, one of the easiest places to project your resistance is out onto your partner. It happens in the blink of an eye. Suddenly your internal anxiety, fear, rage, shame, distress, or sense of disconnection no longer has *anything* to do with you.

It can sound like this: "I would feel happier, more alive, more content *if only* my partner were more loving, emotionally honest, sensitive, a better provider, *or* . . . if my partner were less rigid, controlling, obsessive, or smothering." In this case, the disruption in your energetic awareness comes from focusing your attention outside yourself.

You get the idea. As you are seeing your partner through this narrowed perceptual lens, at least a part of your aliveness process comes to a screeching halt while you wait for *him* or *her* to change. *You have unknowingly given your power away.* When you take back the reins of responsibility for your own happiness, your power returns as well. No matter what the outcome, how you feel about it changes completely when you are holding the reins of your own life.

If you are not married or partnered, it just looks slightly different. The cast of characters changes to your selfish friend or an unappreciative boss or an angry, controlling parent or child.

Remember that in these examples I am pointing out

underlying patterns of the way we judge ourselves and our world and then unconsciously project these judgments outward. The surface content of your particular situation may look different. You are likely to be mixing and matching your own personal collection of behavior patterns.

If Only . . .

Another common form of resistance is to secretly, or not so secretly, wait for the person or job of one's dreams to come along to make us whole and truly happy. This behavior pattern comes in many variations—fear of rejection, impossibly high standards, or fear of commitment or entrapment. In whatever form, it is limiting because we disconnect from our internal experience and dissipate our energy, focusing it out onto the world, looking for that other person or situation that is going to solve our internal distress or loneliness.

Once again, if this is a familiar pattern, you have unknowingly given your power away. When you stop waiting and take back the responsibility for your own happiness, your power returns as well. Opportunities come to you when you are at home in your power—open to receiving what it is you desire.

It's a Cold, Hard World Out There

Then, there are those of us who, based on our past difficult or painful experiences with partnering, decide that the world is indeed *not* a safe place for our heart. So the easiest and least painful route to a sense of wellbeing is to close off those vulnerable parts of ourselves, and go on to excel in other areas, or compensate in some other way. The end result is that we lose internal connection with ourselves by *believing* our fearful projections that belong to the external world. It's not that we haven't had real experiences that create the basis for our perceptions and projections, it's that our *decisions* about those events were made while looking through a narrowed, filtered lens. And once again, energy loss naturally follows when we close off part of ourselves in this way.

The most extreme form of resistance, because of its hallmark of denial, which makes it the most difficult to recognize clearly, is addictions. All addictions—from excessive drinking or eating, gambling, compulsive spending, working, internet surfing, or even excessive exercising—are ways to escape painful or unacceptable internal sensations. Even milder forms of addiction, such as over-scheduling your life or procrastination, serve the same purpose. Remember, these may also be at the root of any disrupted body presence you may be experiencing.

At one level, denial alone, with or without addiction, is another powerful form of resistance. We all have the parts of ourselves and our lives that we don't feel comfortable acknowledging and owning up to.

Can You See the Forest for the Trees?

When we can stand back a bit from our problems to seek a broader perspective, we can see that the underlying cause of much of our resistance boils down to one cause: our beliefs. Our beliefs about ourselves and the world. These are, for the most part, handed down (blindly accepted and internalized) from our families, communities and culture. Our narrowed, hand-me-down beliefs cloud the perceptual lens through which we view the world.

It is important to keep in mind that no matter what our issue or problem seems to be, we are unlikely to be seeing it "as it is." Our narrowed view is selectively closed off to people and places, concepts and opinions, ideas and solutions that don't fit within the scope of our lens. We cannot see what we cannot conceive of or what we reject. Our limiting beliefs see to that. *Exploration III* guides us in how to recognize and let go of those limiting beliefs so that we can see more clearly.

Since we *all* see the world through our own unique and narrowed lens, the deeper answer that this *Exploration* shows us is how to discover and nurture that space of strength and wellbeing *within ourselves*—a place of safety where, layer by layer, we can clean and expand the perceptual lens through which we take in our world—trusting a little more, feeling a little more of ourselves with each step in that direction.

This is what *Exploration III, Healing the Internal Resistance to Life,* is about. Using this *Exploration* allows you to address all forms of resistance, personal and interpersonal, large or small. You can use it to resolve issues and disconnections in interpersonal relationships. You may use it to resolve internal issues and disconnections—all the way down to the most microscopic cellular, DNA, and molecular levels, bringing greater aliveness, joy, and resilience to your everyday experience of living.

As you begin to heal your own places of *internal* fear, denial, and disconnection, *external* disconnections or fearful situations lose their punch. The emotional charge involved in placing your center of wellbeing on others—or external situations—dissolves. You no longer lose energy to your outer world. You regain your internal power to choose.

This means that if your spouse or boss *is* actually abusive in some way, or some other change needs to be instigated in your world, you now have a clear-headed, effective voice to speak up with. You are empowered. You can see what choices you need to make to resolve the situation, and the path unfolds from there. This makes this *Exploration* an excellent adjunct to therapy of any kind: from couples counseling, or individual psychotherapy, to anything in the hands-on healthcare field. You can enhance the therapeutic outcome of any healing session you are receiving if you go into it as an internally informed, empowered person.

How is This Done?

Next, let's look at *how* to unblock obstacles and resistance to your natural energy flow. What are the practical steps in how to regain the sense of connectedness that we *can* have within ourselves—which is our natural state of being: that sense of interconnectedness with the aspects of ourselves that we have inadvertently or consciously pushed away, the places where we tend to go to sleep, the places where we start to judge ourselves or the world around us, creating a sense of separation.

The foundation for *Exploration III* is the strong container that you built doing the grounding and filling in *Exploration II*, as well as the opening awareness of *Exploration I*. I suggest that before proceeding with this session, you go back and repeat those two as many times as needed (over as many days or weeks as needed) until you feel comfortable with the process of filling and energizing yourself—feeling the sense of your body as a container for your energy.

Next, please choose a straightforward instance of physical resistance or distress to work with as a means of introduction to this exercise. Then in the future you can use it to address more complex or seemingly intractable problems.

This will give you a jumpstart as you begin to work with some of the more difficult issues discussed earlier in this chapter, especially if they reside in a very deep core place that you have been locked out of in a mighty, grand way for many years. You may need to repeat this *Exploration* as step-by-step, and layer-by-layer, over days or weeks you regain your capacity to reconnect *fully* with that wounded place.

The key here is to be gentle and kind—*and persistent*—with yourself. With persistent practice of this *Exploration*, you'll continually be *moving in the direction of connection and integration*. With each round of this exercise, as you gently re-establish contact with that core place more and more deeply, you'll feel less disconnected. Trust that you are letting these layers go at a pace that is just right for you.

This process cannot be rushed. Yet, when the moment is right, integration *can* take place in an instant. It can happen that when you repeat this *Exploration*, addressing a particular area of your resistance, that suddenly the last layer dissipates or transforms, and you have the experience of a wonderful rush of energy, of deep connection. Your full, natural energy flow is restored. When this occurs, even if it comes quietly, there's no missing it. This might be *your day* to experience full body presence.

The key to this *Exploration* is to allow yourself to *truly meet* the place(s) inside yourself where you feel a disconnection at some level. As easy as this sounds, we rarely actually do this for ourselves.

We may hover around the spot, getting to know each curve and corner of the edges of our resistance, particularly if it is a place of chronic physical or emotional pain, but to actually *connect* with it is a rare and profound experience.

The only energy I know that truly allows the alchemy of deep transformation to occur is the energy of love. By this I mean 'agape', the ancient all-encompassing, unconditional love of God, Goddess, Christ, Buddha, Great Spirit, or any truly compassionate source of life.

This feeling of love brings us into a deep connection with the Universe. And again, the key is to allow yourself to *deeply feel* this in your body, not to simply visualize it (although it may have visual components).

The energy of love is what causes the ignition of the alchemy of true healing to take place; transforming tight, painful, wounded places into connected, healed components of who we are. When this alchemy is complete, out of our deepest wounds can come our greatest gifts.

So sit quietly for a minute or two and identify an area of physical distress or discomfort. If you don't know what to choose right now, let it go, and you will be given clear guidance on the audio session as to how to find a good spot. *The truth is that anywhere on our path we all have resistance to whatever our next step is going to be.* The good news is that as we practice these *Explorations*, each step along the way gets easier and easier to move through.

Also, *Exploration III* has three segments. You may stop after any of the three segments or go all the way through. The first segment is exploring a physical place of resistance. The second segment is addressing limiting beliefs and painful recurring thoughts. And the third segment is on healing relationships. They are in this order because they build on each other. You will be given the option to stop the session at the end of each segment (signaled by a ten-second period of silence), or you can cruise on through the entire *Exploration*.

Remember, we all work at our own pace and this process cannot be rushed. The starting point for this Exploration *is in having a strong foundation of healthy sensation in your body.*

And then . . .
- Turn your focus inward
- Invite your curiosity to lead the way
- Adopt an open-hearted, nonjudgmental attitude
- Give yourself permission to explore
- Go at your own pace, one that feels comfortable for you
- Allow yourself to simply feel what you feel
- If your mind wanders, gently bring it back
- And, enjoy!

Now that we have set the stage, listen to Exploration III *and then return to this page.*

Now that you have listened to *Exploration III*, let's augment your evaluation with writing in your journal, drawing, moving, or any other expressive way of capturing your experience. The following suggested journal questions may stimulate your thoughts and awareness. Feel free to use them if you find them helpful.

~

Journal Questions

1. What did you notice that was familiar to you in your internal landscape?
2. What surprised you?
3. If you can, describe any sensations, colors, textures, vibration levels, densities, and shapes that showed up during your exploration.
4. What were your dominant thoughts and feelings as you began this check-in?
5. Was there a place in your body where any of those thoughts or feelings were anchored?
6. How did any of that shift or change across the course of the *Exploration*?
7. What stayed the same throughout the *Exploration*?
8. Did any part of your internal landscape inform you of anything that you need to take action on in your life?
9. Was anything a puzzle that you want to percolate on?

~

Allow yourself to truly meet a place inside where you feel a disconnection. This sounds simple, yet the experience is profound.

Chapter 8

∿

Using the Explorations and the Five Principles for
Integration and Renewal

The anecdotal stories and case histories in this chapter have been chosen to reflect a broad spectrum of issues relating to the everyday challenges people experience. What you will read includes personal accounts from people who used the *Explorations* alone, as well as those who had hands-on support during their healing process.

Many nuggets of wisdom are included here in the follow-up discussions about resonance, relationship, power, and presence from the perspective of being a therapist as well as being the client. So even if the problem or issue is not one you are currently experiencing or have experienced in the past, the suggestions may be helpful in other ways.

The stories are arranged by principle because for each one of these people, one of the Five Principles was the entryway to the core of their challenge. Time and again I have been a witness as people used one of these principles as the *first step* that led them to their ultimate healing. After taking that entry door, they often used the other principles and the *Explorations* to go deeper and to ensure that the healing they received held.

At the end of the stories, specific suggestions are offered for you to use to adapt one or more of the *Explorations* to your own needs. From practice and familiarity with this process, you'll easily be able to refocus the version on the audio to reflect the specifics of the issue with which you are working. Also, remember that *Exploration III* has three segments—one segment works with a *physical place* of resistance in your body, one works specifically with *limiting beliefs*, and the third works with *interpersonal relationship issues*. Use these when they would be helpful for your specific issues.

Principle 1

TRUST the Existence of Nurturing Life Energy

Trusting that there is an unlimited source of nourishing, life-giving energy in the Universe allows you to recognize that you are loved, and supported throughout your life, and allows you to live from trust rather than from fear.

The following two examples are experiences where the principle of trust was the entryway for beginning the healing and integration process. While other principles also are included in these stories, Principle 1—Trust was the door opener in these two cases. If this is the principle that calls to you, or that you have encountered in those around you, read on.

My Marriage is a Disaster

Linda came in to see me while feeling extremely hopeless following a separation from her husband. Her abusive, alcoholic husband had been an unhealthy connection in her life for years. She had fallen in love young and calibrated her worth and her abilities by how she judged her. After months of quiet contemplation, Linda had been able to come to the initial decision about ending her marriage. However, within days of her decision, she fell prey to her fears of being on her own, although knowing deep inside that it was the right move. Fears that she could not make it alone in the world, that she might become lost in disconnection and succumb to the deep depressive feelings that tugged at her core. She had worked intensively with her psychotherapist, with whom she had talked about her feelings and recognized intellectually what she needed to do in order to move beyond her fears. Despite this work, she continued to feel torn inside—at times depressed, almost suicidal. She had lost sight of her trust and the inner wisdom that she could be supported in this decision.

In our opening session, we began by working with *Exploration I, Opening Awareness*, so that she could begin to experience her internal landscape and trust her inner wisdom. As I sat with her, she closed her eyes, took her awareness inside her body, and began to identify where in her body she felt the source of her depression. As she became quiet and listened closely, it became clear that it was coming from a tightly coiled place in her belly. Inside the tight coil, she was able to identify a part of her that still felt like the small, abused child she had once been. As she reconnected with this child part of herself, it expressed the feeling that "she was not good enough and not strong enough to survive in the world alone." The small child within told her that even though her marriage was a disaster and drained her, it was at least *some* connection. As she listened to the voice of this child-self, she knew it was the source of the doubt she had been experiencing about her ability to create new, healthier relationships—to connect to healthy resources and let go of the unhealthy ones.

As I listened, I realized that this fearful part of Linda had long ago lost touch with the healthy support available to her. Her ability to trust in any support was minimal.

In response to this, I consciously increased my own therapeutic presence for her to energetically connect with and receive from when she was ready. I did this by relaxing more fully in my own body while maintaining our connection. I used my energetic awareness as I checked in with how my spine felt against the chair I was seated in. I then dropped my attention to my lower back and legs. I continued to ground and fill, feeling the stability of the earth beneath my feet as we worked. I let my full body presence spread out and create a soft, non-invasive cushion of energy so she could feel safe *and* supported. As I did this, I felt better and better as well.

Next, she looked inside for a place where she felt *some* sense of connection to her core truth, her inner strength. She described a presence in her heart, a sense of a 'clear-headed woman', that was a source of strength to her. She had been talking with her psychotherapist about this aspect of herself, but hadn't really *felt* this part or its power to help her move forward in her life.

Gently, I asked her a series of questions that guided her to sense how she could connect to healthy resources and receive external support for the 'clear-headed woman' in her heart.

"What sensation, from the rich energy field of the earth, would feel most nourishing coming in through your feet and legs?" We sat quietly together and I grounded with her as she began to feel some sensation happening there and moving on up into her torso.

Next I asked, "Can you feel a sense of nurturing from the warmth of the sunlight pouring in through the window behind you onto your back?"

This healthy resource was very palpable to her. She immediately began to feel the back of her neck and her ribcage relaxing and spreading out. Soon, she noticed that her chest area was beginning to fill with a warm, tingling sensation that spread down to her belly and met the warmth coming up from her legs.

She had systematically accessed two external resources: the feeling of the earth's steadiness coming into her feet and legs, and the sensation of gentle warmth from the sunlight on her back.

Once she felt connected and filled by these healthy resources throughout her whole body, I asked her to notice how the 'clear-headed woman' in her heart was feeling in relation to the little girl part. She said that the woman felt huge and strong and that the 'little abused girl' was quiet and peaceful, having made her way into the arms of the strong woman in her heart. She described her physical body as though it were vastly wider and deeper than her actual physical boundaries. She was experiencing full body presence.

She felt very aware of all parts of herself and was delighted that she did not need to exclude any of them because of their intense feelings. All her emotions and feelings were honored and given a voice. Her core wisdom and her fear were both heard and given a chance to be expressed and nurtured by the connections inside and outside of herself. I recognized that her navigational system was operational again—perhaps for the first time in her adult life.

Linda ended the session with a deeper understanding of her situation. By learning to trust that healthy resources were all around her, and to recognize several of them in our session, she was able to fill up the container of her being, giving her a sense of full body presence that she had never had before. From there, healing and integration naturally occurred as her inner wisdom was empowered to act on her behalf. Her perceptual lens expanded to include new possibilities she had never experienced before.

She walked away from the session, knowing she could self-catalyze this process again if necessary by choosing healthy, life-giving resources, rather than falling back into the old self-sabotaging habits. As long as we live and walk on the planet, these kinds of healthy resources are always available to us.

After the session, Linda continued to work with *Exploration II,* grounding and filling herself on a daily basis. This kept her in close contact with her body's internal landscape and able to navigate through her world feeling more connected to her full body presence.

Linda's experience reminds us all that by developing access to our own source of inner wisdom and nourishing ourselves with what we need, we can create intimacy and strengthen the relationship with ourselves on all levels.

~

Specific Suggestions

Learning to *Trust the Existence of Nurturing Life Energy* was the doorway for Linda. Know that your entry point may differ. If you are someone who knows what you should be doing to lead a healthy and fulfilling life, but something inside consistently sabotages your desires and keeps you from taking actions in a healthy direction, the following suggestions may be valuable:

1. Start with listening to *Exploration I* with your goal being to discern where your internal awareness is calling you. Notice what emotions or feelings may be there.

2. While the emotions or sensations are fully present, listen for a limiting belief, or an image to emerge, to guide you to which principle will be your doorway into deeper discovery. Let your navigational system lead you.

3. Use *Explorations II and III* to support and catalyze the uncovering and releasing of limiting beliefs and trapped traumatic energy, both of which can prevent you from healing.

4. Repeat all three *Explorations* as needed, particularly if the patterns are lifelong or deeply imprinted. In this case, this process is best done in layers so that it is not overwhelming and can be better integrated as things heal. Often it is most effective to deal with longstanding issues with a grounded facilitator of some kind.

Lost My Job After Years of Devoted Service

One of my long-time students, Stefan, told me about a time when he was suddenly dismissed from a job where he had put in many years of devoted service. Initially, Stefan was devastated—his usual competent presence was completely disrupted. He felt as though all his hard work had gone unseen and unappreciated, and, consequently, his self-esteem was at an all-time low. He felt totally alone in his fear that he was somehow fundamentally flawed. As he tells the story, the numb sensation in his gut turned into a deep ache. As the hours passed, he knew he should move or take some restorative action, but he was still in shock, truly believing that this dismissal meant that he was a total failure. He knew it wasn't rational to feel this way, but he could not shake it. The experience was paralyzing for him.

Then a friend's chance phone call reminded him of the first principle about *Trusting the Existence of Nurturing Life Energy*. In remembering to trust that he *could* be supported, he realized he didn't have to carry this abysmal event alone. This helped him to break through his wall of painful isolation and speak to his friend truthfully about how he was feeling. In doing this, he was allowing his friend into what was really happening rather than trying to pretend that everything was okay. His friend's listening ear and open heart offered Stefan a therapeutic presence to connect with. Stefan *chose a healthy resource for himself* rather than staying mired in the shock of the dismissal. When the call was done, Stefan noticed he felt a *little* better. He had shared honestly with his friend and with that he started to refill. From there—remembering *Exploration II*—he stopped, tuned in further, and took the time to ground and fill, connecting to his internal landscape and offering it nourishing sensations, as best he could in that moment.

Remembering to *trust the existence of nurturing life energy,* even when he was having a difficult time *feeling* it, was his doorway into gathering other healthy resources. Resources such as remembering a time when someone he admired greatly had been through a similar situation and had bounced back with more strength and success than ever. In fact, this admired mentor had used the situation to make a major career change. Stefan imagined what his mentor would do, how he would act, if he were in Stefan's current situation. He said it was almost as though his 'admired someone' was right there in the room with him, brainstorming. So *expanding his perceptual lens* was the next doorway in his healing process. Ideas began to pop into his awareness as he opened to new ways of looking at his situation. He also called other friends and colleagues who reminded him of his strengths, expanding his lens on himself even more. By the end of the day, the aching and numbness in his gut had faded. He was able to feel the ground under his feet again and his steadiness was returning. He knew he had the resources and could find his way to new possibilities from there.

As the weeks passed and he explored new potential jobs, Stefan used *Exploration III* as a resource. Whenever the remnants of numbness and aching, or the limiting belief that he was somehow fundamentally flawed, would show up, he would use them as a signal to stop, tune in, and use *Exploration III* to release and resolve the next layer. Slowly he regained his full body presence. He was able to feel more and more nurturing energy in his body as he integrated the sensation of this life-giving energy throughout his entire system. This made it easier to discern and then choose what resources would be most helpful in keeping him on track and moving toward his full potential. His confidence in his skills and abilities became stronger every day.

He now has a new job—one that suits him better, in a much healthier work environment. He is getting to use his creativity and talents in a more satisfying way. He has learned to choose healthy resources that keep him connected to his deep strength and steadiness. And he has the knowledge that he has the resilience to bounce back, and even end up in a better place.

Specific Suggestions

Trusting the Existence of Nurturing Life Energy was the first step for Stefan. Recall that your entry point may differ. Notice that he then proceeded to expanding his perceptual lens and move on through all the rest of the principles. This naturally happens in many circumstances, and all you need to do is recognize one of the principles to catalyze the process.

If you have recently experienced a devastating event (e.g., losing your job or the death of a loved one), this may have triggered one or more of your most crippling, limiting beliefs. This is not unusual at all. Often they are not rational nor reasonable. They are usually from your past history, completely outdated in their message to you—but seriously disruptive of your presence nonetheless. The following suggestions may be of help to you:

1. If you are trapped in a limiting belief, a helpful first step is to stop. Then tune in, and ground and fill. Imagine that your best friend, trusted mentor, or another knowledgeable and loving figure is right there with you in the room.

2. Imagine they have found themselves in a situation similar to yours. From financial devastation to a sudden break up, to loss of a job or position, or to death of a loved one; we each have these things happen from time to time.

3. Allow yourself to brainstorm with them, as Stefan did, as to how they would find their way beyond this situation you are stuck in.

4. Identify which principle is your first step and which *Exploration* would be most beneficial to begin healing.

Alternate Suggestions

1. An alternative is to imagine that your best friend or a good client is in the room with you; stuck in the dilemma you are experiencing. You counsel them on how to move beyond it.

2. How could your friend or client expand his or her perceptual lens to see this issue differently?

3. Would this person believe the limiting belief that you are feeling stuck in? If not, what would he say to himself to move beyond it? Can you say that to yourself?

4. How would this person solve the issue at hand? What principle could he use? Which *Exploration* would benefit him most?

To Explore Further

1. Who in your world can you actually reach out to at this time to help you expand your perceptual lens? Can you reach them by phone or in person? Perhaps write them an email or a letter, asking for what you need.

2. Be pro-active. Let whoever you are asking know that you need help moving beyond a specific limiting belief. For instance, if you recently experienced a break-up and are feeling unlovable and not good enough, ask a friend to remind you of all the ways you are good enough and lovable. Sure, you may have made mistakes that contributed to the break-up, but first you need to get your full container back again so you can see the situation and hear the feedback more clearly. So connect to resources that will refill you.

3. Utilize all the *Explorations*, as you need them to get the navigational system of your being up and fully operational again—to recover your full body presence.

~

Trusting *the Existence of Nurturing Life Energy* is a key feature in healing and creating what we want in our worlds.

As you can see from these examples, it can be invoked even when the *feeling* of trust is not there yet. So in whatever way you can get in the door and move towards being able to feel that trust in the process is ultimately helpful and life giving. From this point all the other principles of *choosing, feeling, integrating,* and *expanding* follow easily.

Notice that the examples and suggestions that follow these two experiences are different in that one is learning to trust within yourself and one is bridging to external resources to help initiate the feeling of trust. These are about two significant aspects of the principle of *Trust*. Since Stefan's disruption was triggered in the external realm, he chose to begin his healing process by reaching out into his external world. Linda's disruption of full body presence was buried within and so she chose to connect with and integrate on an inner level initially.

~

Principle 2

FEEL the Presence of Life Energy in Your Body

Feeling your internal connection to this life energy, as a natural state of being, opens your awareness to discover a sense of belonging, reclaim your inner wisdom, and experience vitality and joy.

The following three examples are experiences where the principle of *Feeling the Presence of Life Energy in Your Body* was the entryway for beginning the healing and integration process. Other principles also are included in these stories, but *Feeling* was the door opener in these two cases. If this principle calls to you, or you have encountered it in those around you, read on.

Feeling My Tumor

Ben has always been a concrete, left-brained kind of guy. When he first arrived in my office, he was only there because someone he trusted referred him. He had recently had surgery to remove a completely encapsulated nine-pound cancerous tumor from his abdomen. This slender, fit man hadn't noticed there was anything wrong until the tumor was almost full size.

As his story unfolded, it became clear that he had a touch deficit that left him with limited capacity to feel much internally below his neck. Growing up in an affluent family, his care had been left to a nursemaid who neglected him and gave him very little touch. His memories of his hours alone in his crib left him numb.

I knew I had to begin by helping him learn how to sense his own body's internal landscape. Because he doubted himself in this area, he initially worked to suspend all judgment of what he was capable of feeling and *imagined* he could feel *anything* inside himself. We played a lot with how different parts of him felt compared to other parts, "Does it feel more dense in your chest or your belly?", until he realized he *was capable* of sensing his internal landscape and that he could feel quite a lot.

He worked with *Exploration I, Opening Awareness*, and *Exploration II, Grounding and Filling*, a number of times until he began to have a lot more sensation. After one particular grounding and filling, he asked me, "Is it possible that bringing in nourishing energy could re-grow my tumor?" I asked him what he felt. During the *Exploration*, he suddenly sensed a tiny nub of a growth in his gut where the other tumor had been removed. I suggested that he could be sensing something important and that he might want to see his oncologist to get it checked out. It was indeed, exactly as he *felt* it internally. And they went back in and surgically removed the tiny bit of tumor long before it was a problem.

He was ultimately reassured to know that he could feel that keenly and stay healthy! In addition, as his capacity to feel his internal landscape increased, his capacity to trust his energetic awareness increased as well.

We then worked with *Exploration III* so he could hold his gut area with those internal energy hands in an unconditional, loving manner, so that it stayed a healthy, energy-filled place where his immune system was more able to patrol the area and keep it safe. This meant cancer cells would have a much harder time taking hold and proliferating. We checked in regularly with his system to make sure that he was still clear, and he felt more and more confident with his abilities as time passed.

∽

Specific Suggestions

Feeling the Presence of Life Energy in Your Body was the first step for Ben. Remember your entry point may differ. This following suggestions are especially helpful for those who were neglected as children or those who have experienced physical trauma that has left them with reduced bodily sensation due to frozen, numb, or painful places. These are places of severe disruption in your body presence. If you have a hard time feeling your body's internal landscape—your insides—for any reason, the following specific suggestions may be very helpful.

Set up time to practice with *Explorations I and II* regularly. Daily is optimal. While using *Exploration I*, if sensation 'hits' are eluding you, try the following strategies:

1. Compare density, weight, and color qualities *between* different areas of your body. For instance, you could ask yourself:
   a) "Does my chest area feel lighter or darker than my belly?"
   b) "Does my head feel heavier or lighter than my chest?"
   c) "Which feels denser, my right leg or my left leg?"
   d) "Does my spine feel fuller or more empty than the rest of my torso?"

2. Ask yourself about different qualities in a specific area. Such as: "If my heart felt like a color, would it be orange-

111

red or blue-green or brown-red or some other color?"

3.   Once you have asked yourself one of these questions, allow the answer to pop in quickly. Listen to your first hit. Whatever comes is right. Do not edit or judge your answer. Just let it drop into your conscious awareness and acknowledge it. It's fun. Only you know the answers. You just didn't know you knew them until now.

4.   Take time now to record your sensations by writing in a journal, drawing, or painting. A few minutes of recording in this way can really bring these elusive sensations to a more concrete level.

5.   When you find that you are feeling more sensations with *Exploration I,* without all the extra questions, you can let go of these extra steps and move on to *Exploration II, Grounding and Filling.* You will probably have an easier time with identifying nourishing, nurturing sensations for yourself, now that you have sharpened up your inner awareness skills. Also, important sensation clues—such as what happened for Ben—can now naturally drop into your conscious awareness as you are doing *Exploration II.*

Parenting My Volatile Child

Melinda is the mother of Justin, a sweet-hearted but very volatile child with mild autism. Justin has difficulties processing through his sensory system. The result is he constantly feels bombarded with smells, sounds, and visual stimuli in his world. He alternately withdraws completely into his own world or has loud temper tantrums that leave Melinda feeling exhausted and overwhelmed.

When I first met Melinda, she was sitting in one of my classes, with her legs tucked up under her, lotus-style. As we began, I asked everyone to place both feet on the floor to start grounding and filling. She looked surprised, but complied immediately. However, the first chance she got, her legs were tucked up under her again. Later, as people began to share their experiences, a woman next to her welled up with tears. Although she was being polite, I could tell Melinda was agitated by the emotion being expressed. In fact, I could sense her getting more uncomfortable as each moment passed. I quietly asked her to put her feet back on the floor and to ground one more time down into the earth's energy field.

Melinda later shared her experience in that moment:

> Suddenly I was remembering when I was a child and my parents argued viciously with each other. One time when I was about eight years old, watching TV on the family room couch, my parents really got into a huge argument in front of me. I wanted to curl up and disappear. In fact, now that I think about it, I *did energetically* curl up and disappear—my body presence was seriously disrupted—so that they would not notice me and yell at *me*. My brother got the bulk of their attention because he fought back. He fared *far* worse than I did. So my defensive strategy worked really well for me *then*, but it wasn't working in the class, and I suddenly realized it certainly does not work with my son and his need to have me stay steady, calm *and present*—not disappearing.
>
> I've been shrinking away from *feeling* my legs and feet, away from his volatility, and disappearing for years. It has

been exhausting to survive that way. And here I was doing it again in the class! So I trusted the process and allowed myself to expand downward and *feel nurturing sensation* in my legs and feet for the first time that I can remember. It felt weird at first and a little scary, but I did it anyway and very quickly it felt better.

Melinda visibly relaxed, as she was able to feel her feet and legs in a good way again. She was reclaiming her full body presence. I could sense that she felt steadier and safer. Her face softened. Her shoulders dropped. Her spine rested back against her chair. The emotional sharing in the room no longer bothered her. In fact, she reported feeling *more* connected to the other people in the room without feeling agitated or ungrounded.

If she were an object rather than a person, I would say that the flow of life's energy, like electricity, now has a ground, a connection that makes it more manageable and less scary. She is no longer about to be 'fried' by the emotional 'charge' in the room or by her old emotionally charged memories.

Weeks later Melinda tells me,

The interesting thing is, now that I am living more in my legs and feet, feeling the earth under me, I can stay therapeutically present with my son and he is *much calmer.* He is having fewer emotional swings. I hadn't realized it before, but it's as though his emotional mood swings and volatility were his way of responding to my lack of full body presence with him, in the only way he knew how.

As we talk even later, she shares this:

As a long-time practitioner of yoga and meditation, I had cultivated a clear sense of how to calm my nervous system using my yoga breathing and meditation. However, I couldn't hold it for very long outside of my meditation room. I could be calm while still and alone, but not in the fray of my life as the mother of a special needs child. Since the class and work with the *Explorations*, I have been practicing putting my feet on the floor and connecting and filling up as often as I can during my day, and I have noticed I am consistently more able to *walk in my world* and feel that sense of being full and steady.

People's opinions don't sway me the way they used to. I can tolerate and even enjoy certain situations in my life that I could not before. I can now have a flow of nourishing energy *all the way through my body*, not just from the base of my spine on up through my torso. And as I establish a full container, my presence gets bigger and life feels easier.

Looking back, I realize that my old 'shrinking' habit cut off the flow of the energy from the earth through my legs and feet. And when I shrank, anyone's emotional process around me felt really overwhelming. Once I learned how to reconnect, I felt more of my internal landscape. I could be in different, new situations and enjoy them—even learn from them. As the mother of a special needs child with lots of emotional ups and downs, this is having a huge impact!

Also, my resilience is better. I know *when* to slow down and rest, and I can go for longer periods of time without resting. I have more stamina. Somehow, having a nice strong sense of my feet and legs connected to the ground under me, gives me the support I have never had before.

Melinda's son did not miraculously become a model child because of her newfound steadiness, but what did happen was that Justin became significantly calmer. When things did come up that upset him, because she felt her body and was fully present, she could trust her capacity to hold a therapeutic presence and choose healthier resources. She was then more able to respond in ways that were helpful and useful to him and everyone else, rather than operating from a disrupted body presence, and feeling overwhelmed by "his needs and his noise," as she called it. She also began *standing her ground* and speaking up for herself in the rest of the family. Initially, this caused waves, but as she stayed steady and connected to the needs of everyone (including herself), things slowly got a lot smoother and happier.

Melinda shared more six months later:

> I am astonished at how much closer I feel to my son and husband these days. We actually have times that I could define as fun—even joyful—sweet moments of connection that I have never felt before. I am realizing I had been living my life at a functional level, but constantly on red alert, waiting for Justin's volatility to erupt. So, I was never really able to relax. Reclaiming my connection to the earth through my feet and legs was pivotal for me. Once I had a sense of the ground under me on a consistent basis, I just felt steadier, more relaxed. When I go back and remember those years as a kid, all curled up and small, I know that person *was* me, but it doesn't have to be me for the rest of my life! I am back in school getting my master's degree, following through on a life-long dream. I am moving forward in my world, rather than disappearing. It feels so much better.

Feeling her body was Melinda's first step, and the effect on her and her family was life changing.

∽

Specific Suggestions

Feeling the Presence of Life Energy in Your Body was the first step for Melinda. If you are someone who has not been in the lower half of your body much, or you do not feel a friendly, easy connection with the earth's energy field for some reason, you may find the following suggestions valuable. This would apply to anyone who tends to live in their head, or who has a tendency to contract under stress, pulling in tightly or pulling up and out of their body under stress.

This may also be valuable for someone like me who has years of experience doing yoga, and meditating in the seated lotus position. In yoga I was taught to concentrate on bringing energy from the base of my spine up and out the crown, or to circulate the life force in my torso. In doing so, I was totally bypassing my legs and feet and their connection to the earth. So I had a strong presence when I was meditating but not in walking in my world. If this sounds familiar read on.

1. Start with *Exploration I* to ascertain where you are comfortable and present in your body and where you are not as present. Be curious, not judgmental.

2. Practice *Exploration II* to connect and fill up. Then work with *Exploration III* to hold in a loving way—to reclaim—the parts of yourself you are locked out of or not inhabiting for some reason. Please be sure that your feet are in contact with the earth as you do this.

3. Usually, as you move back into the parts of yourself that you were not as present in, the reason for the disruption in your presence will show up in some form. This may take the form of a spontaneous memory like Melinda had, or perhaps a dream recalled later that tells the story. I encourage you to journal when you identify a disruption—sometimes it will emerge as you journal in a stream of consciousness manner after the *Exploration*.

4. Commit to working with all three *Explorations* on a regular basis until all the layers of the old habit have been released. This will give you back a much steadier sense of the totality of yourself, so that you can walk in your world with your power and full body presence.

Burned-Out from Caring for My Elderly Mom

Sandra is the primary caregiver for her elderly mother, Edna. She moved back in with her three years ago to care for her following her mother's stroke. Edna has been difficult to handle due to her own life-long fearfulness, on top of her physical neediness after the stroke. She insists that Sandra do everything for her and won't allow anyone else to come in to cook or clean. Sandra's life has been sorely curtailed as she has tried to take adequate care of her mom.

We began by doing *Exploration I, Opening Awareness*, and she dissolved into tears of frustration as she realized how empty she felt. Her spine was tight. Her heart felt like a closed fist. Her bones felt empty to her. She really was at rock bottom on many levels. From this place, her mom's fear was running both their lives. Sandra was no longer clear about what she herself needed.

We went immediately to *Exploration II, Grounding and Filling*, and really took our time to fill every nook and cranny of her system. When we completed that *Exploration*, her bones felt much juicier, and she had a small cushion of energy with which to work. Her tears stopped and she was feeling steadier. However, her heart still felt closed to her. So we proceeded to *Exploration III*, so that her heart could be held by loving, unconditional energy. As she held her heart, a younger version of her emerged and the tears began again.

> I just want to please her—I have tried so hard all my life to please her and nothing is ever good enough. No matter how much I do, she is still critical. I just want her to love and appreciate me.

More tears. As the wave of tears washed through her, she slowly relaxed. Her heart was softening. Her face was more open. She had reclaimed a part of herself. As the tears stopped, I asked how her heart felt.

"The fist is looser now, but I need to get it open all the way. It still hurts—less now, but it still hurts."

I asked her to notice how her backbone felt behind her heart. As she felt her spine, I felt her chest expanding bit by bit. Then I asked her to feel her sitting bones on the chair. She relaxed even more. I asked her to feel her feet making contact with the earth again. I could sense her system steadying out.

I asked Sandra what her younger self would like to say to the Sandra of today.

She is no longer crying. She just needs to be held. The adult in me knows that my mother is like a wounded little kid who never grew up. But my younger self was still wanting her to mother me the way a mother should—to love me unconditionally and support me and tell me I am wonderful. I never got that.

This realization expanded her perceptual lens as she held the possibility of experiencing her mother more accurately.

She was silent for a few minutes.

"She is not capable of giving me that, is she?"

I concurred. She looked sadder, but somehow more at peace. I asked her what her younger self wanted to be doing in her life if she weren't worried about pleasing her mother. She was silent again, but a smile was growing on her face as her perceptual lens expanded even more.

I would want to go dancing again with my friends like I used to do. I would want to go watch the sunset on the beach. I would call my college roommates and go to dinner. I would take an entire afternoon to read my favorite novel and listen to my favorite music.

She was really on a roll here. I let her keep going as her full body presence returned. We brainstormed about how to get competent help to stay with her mom so she could get time away. Initially, she was not as sure of this aspect of the plan, but she practiced being grounded and full as she spoke with her mom and laid out the plan to get help. She was steady and clear as she left the session.

One week later, she was back. She listened to *Exploration II,*

Grounding and Filling, every day, and also just before she talked with her mom, so that she could go into the interchange with full body presence. Her mom went into her normal fearful, clingy response when Sandra announced that she had arranged for a highly recommended nurse to take her place the following week for several hours every day.

> I was pleasantly surprised by how steady I felt. I could clearly see her for the scared little girl that she is inside, rather than the tyrannical boss I have let her be all these years! As I continued to hold a strong therapeutic presence, and she saw that I was not backing down, she quieted down. We were able to talk about it in civil way. She did get manipulative again the next morning, but I stayed grounded and she eventually backed down that time as well. By the third time, when she started her old routine the following day, I was firmly in my full body presence, and it hardly lasted any time at all. I know she is still afraid, but she seems less so as I stay steady and clear about my decisions. I think that during all of these years, I have been joining her in her fear. Now she seems to be joining me in my steadiness. It is great!

I shared with Sandra how when you put several working pendulums in a room together, they all eventually come into synchrony with the largest one. In other words, the largest energy presence in the room prevails. I encouraged her to continue to be the largest presence in the room every time she is with her mother. She was pleasantly surprised to find that when she changed the energy dynamic in their relationship, everything else shifted with it. It took some effort and commitment to change her habit of shrinking in the presence of

121

her mother, but once she was able to stay connected to healthy resources and be a larger, steadier presence, everything changed.

Life is getting more interesting every week for Sandra. She is practicing holding her ground and being the largest presence in the room over and over again as her mom tries unsuccessfully to get back the control in their relationship. She is taking more time for herself and getting back her life, day by day. The hidden benefit is that she is bringing her full body presence into the other areas of her life as well. So she is enjoying everything in her life more every day. The principle of *Feeling the Presence of Life Energy in Your Body* has given Sandra back her life. From there, her perceptual lens has expanded, and she is choosing healthy resources moment to moment in order to maintain full body presence.

⁓

Specific Suggestions

Feeling the Presence of Life Energy in Your Body was Sandra's first step. If you are exhausted from caring for an aging or ill family member, or if you find yourself subject to manipulation by others, the following suggestions will be valuable for you:

1. Regular (daily) practice of *Exploration II* is the key. You want to get to a point where it is a habit to be living your life from a full container. Your wisest decisions are made when your container is full and connected to healthy resources.

2. Use *Exploration III* to discover where you are losing energy. Sandra was losing energy to the younger version

of herself that desperately wanted her mom's approval. She could not make a wise decision about her life, or her mom's life, as long as that part of her was 'driving her bus'. Her full body presence was clearly disrupted. In holding her younger self in a loving manner, she was able to resolve this issue. She continues to have conversations with this part of herself when she starts to feel stressed or contracted again. This child part was basically operating from the limiting belief that she was not worth taking care of—only pleasing her mom and getting her mom's approval could make her feel good enough about herself. She had to release that belief and step back into her power to resolve this. Find the limiting belief you are losing energy to and work to resolve it, *Exploration III, Segment 2,* can help you with this.

3. Tune into your inner wisdom, and ask what you need to be doing in your life to rejuvenate and care for yourself. This could be a regular group you belong to, a form of exercise that makes you feel good, or any number of other things. Ask internally, discover what nurturing, nourishing self-care you need, and commit to putting it in your life day to day. And, then, *do* it.

4. Keep track of when you start to contract or feel an energetic disruption in your body. Commit to practices that keep you as the 'largest presence' in the care-giving process while also taking care of yourself.

～

Feeling the Presence of Life Energy in Your Body is an essential element in healing and connecting with your inner wisdom—which is a vital component of your navigational system.

Ben's ability to feel his abdomen, Melinda learning to feel her legs and feet, and Sandra feeling more energy in her heart— these were the initial and primary actions required for transforming their lives. From this point, all the other principles of choosing, trusting, integrating, and expanding follow easily.

Each of these three people derived different benefits from this principle. Ben gained a clear sense of his internal landscape and his inner wisdom that saved his life. Melinda gained a sense of belonging in her feet and legs, which led to a greater sense of belonging in her full body presence with her family and the world. Sandra regained her vitality and joy as she learned how to feel her full body presence and create a life separate from her mother's fear. They all discovered how much easier and more natural it is when life is experienced from inside their bodies.

～

Principle 3

INTEGRATE this Energy
Throughout Your Entire System.

*Integrating a felt sense of this nurturing energy
throughout your entire body helps you establish
a full personal container with strong,
flexible healthy boundaries.*

T he following two examples are experiences where the principle of *Integrating this Energy throughout Your Entire System* was the entryway for beginning the healing and transformation process. Other principles are also included in these stories, but *Integrating* was the door opener in these two cases. If *Integrating* is the principle that calls to you, or that you have encountered in those around you, read on.

I'm Not Afraid of Hard Work

Julie is a sharp, intelligent woman. She is in management in the corporate world. Quiet and focused, she is able to really make things happen. She has mastered how to get the job done. She grew up on a farm and is not afraid of hard work. In fact, working hard is her primary default stance in life. Ask her to do something or learn something and she will immediately jump in and work *very hard* to succeed. Straight-ahead focus; go for the goal. She has spent most of her life pulled forward, anticipating the next moment.

Julie's motto is, "Give me a job, and I plow right into it—I'm not afraid of hard work."

In the course of a bodywork session with me, Julie was trying to slow down and let her awareness and her presence spread out, allowing her to be more relaxed and diffuse. At one point, she was trying to bring her energetic awareness—her presence—into a place in her gut where she could not feel much energy.

She chuckled and said, "There I go again, working hard at relaxing and spreading out!"

She realized her work was actually to back off, let go of the goal and let her softening awareness just *be* there, without trying to *do* anything.

As my hands were cradling her gut, I recognized that 'not afraid of hard work' was a default stance for me as well. Throughout my life I have constantly brought this default stance to my conscious attention and made a decision to relax and let go.

I know that I am not alone in this. In my experience of teaching thousands of students, I would say that many people operate out of this default stance. The phrase, "If you want to get something done, give it to a busy person", came from somewhere! And, the invisible, fundamental mandate of 'working hard'—moving into action, and staying there for most of my waking hours—gives me a sense of completion and competence, but it doesn't do much for my ability to simply *be present* in each moment. I am stuck in a *doing* mode if I am living from this default stance. When this is the case, it is hard to enjoy my life. It is hard to be anywhere but in the future when I am 'working hard': thinking about how much I am getting done, thinking about how happy I'll be when I get finished, how accomplished I will feel, how others will be happy with what I have accomplished.

So, how could I facilitate Julie's healing and perhaps my own? First, I committed to holding a space for her that held no judgment and was kind and loving. We laughed together, and I let my hands on her gut get even softer and more present, more melded with her. I committed to simply *be* a full body presence for her, which would allow her to do the same with herself. To do this, I knew I must be clear and present in myself as best I could in that moment.

I could not be secretly judging myself. I could not be 'working hard' to have her relax. I could not have an agenda for her. I needed to simply be present with her as she learned for herself, and from my therapeutic presence, how to relax and let go of the goal. This was fun. I had to relax in order to help her learn to relax. I liked this. We both started giggling and then laughing and then really laughing at how we normally thought we needed to focus so hard in our work in order to survive and succeed. Our stomachs hurt, we were laughing so hard. It felt really good.

When Julie and I were able to relax, we both felt as though our boundaries were more flexible and healthier—our containers more full and with an easier flow of nurturing life energy. The sharp focus that we were both so familiar with had softened, and we had opened to more joy and laughter.

At the end of the session Julie reported feeling more energetic awareness throughout her entire system. I felt great. It had been a groundbreaking session for her. She had attained a sense of ease she had never experienced before. I felt full and happy. This was one of those sessions where to give truly was to receive.

~

Specific Suggestions

Julie's first step was to *integrate* a sense of relaxation *throughout her entire system*. If you are the kind of person who works really hard in life, has a difficult time relaxing, or spends a lot of time thinking about the future, the following suggestions may be valuable:

1. *Exploration II* is the key here. Filling up regularly and allowing yourself to meet your world in a full and relaxed manner is crucial to creating grace and ease in your life. For a better balance between work and rest, while you are grounding and filling, ask your system— your body and mind—specifically what it needs to slow down and rest. Observe how your cells and tissues respond to the questions about slowing down. One of my favorite questions in this category is to ask how my favorite massage therapist's hands would feel resting on my shoulders. If I feel my shoulders drop significantly with that question, I know I need to slow down and get a massage.

2. If you are trying to discern exactly what direction would be best for slowing down, ask your *insides* questions that involve possible activities such as a really good massage, a long, warm soak in a mineral bath overlooking the Pacific ocean at Esalen, a day or a week or a month off with nothing in the schedule, slow-dancing to your favorite music, petting your cat or dog, sharing a cup of coffee

with a friend—you get the idea. See how you feel inside as you imagine yourself doing those activities. Then you can either schedule something for yourself, or, if it is not within practical range, you can continue to soak it up through your mind's eye and all your other parts that know how to take in nurturing sensation. You can tell by your internal response what your next step should be.

3. Until I was in a really relaxed, slower, healthier space, I could not conceive of how to proceed in my life without the 'work hard' default stance driving me. Once I slowed down enough to feel what daily rhythm actually nourished me, I could make better choices in my life. Some people have to 'crash and burn' to figure out that over-working isn't healthy for them, but I highly recommend the 'choose to slow down and take a deeper look' approach. And, honestly, once you are doing the Grounding and Filling in *Exploration II* on a daily basis, your inner wisdom will begin to speak to you about what pace is healthiest for you.

4. Take time off to engage in activities that are relaxing and energizing at the same time. From weekend to month-long retreats, weekly meditation or yoga classes, religious services or retreats that allow you to slow down and have time for inward reflection—all of these can be nourishing resources for people who have the default stance of working too hard and forgetting to "stop and smell the roses." Life is too short to miss the good stuff that we can only perceive and receive when we have slowed down enough take it in.

Teenage Daughter's Power Struggle

Mary and her 14-year-old daughter, Kelly, are constantly at odds. When Mary asks her daughter questions about her plans for the evening, or her life in general, Kelly feels controlled and manipulated. Mary just wants to know that her daughter is safe and taking care of herself. Kelly pulls away and gets evasive in response to feeling controlled. Mary then worries that Kelly is hiding something, that she is actually doing something dangerous or stupid. This dynamic gets played out multiple times in any given week. They both are miserable when they arrive at my door.

I begin by explaining to Kelly that our session is about her getting her power in her relationship with her mother. She likes that idea, but I can tell she is still wary of me. Her mom has known me for a number of years, and Kelly is not yet sure where my loyalties lie. I go on to explain to her that in this session I will give them both a set of skills that will help them navigate their relationship so that it feels like a win-win situation rather than the lose-lose one they are operating from right now. She tells me she is willing to give it a try.

First, I ask them to sit facing each other, a comfortable distance apart. I ask each of them to close their eyes and we do *Exploration I* to get a baseline sensation to work from. Afterward, Kelly shares that she feels "fine" and "normal." Mary is more truthful. She shares that she is realizing that her energy presence is leaning toward Kelly, taking up all the air space between them. Her energetic awareness is out in front of her, not integrated throughout her entire system. When Kelly hears what her mom is saying, her face lights up and she says, "I can feel that! Like a pressure on my chest—back off Mom."

Mary responds to the feedback by working to get her

energy presence to return to her own body and integrate it throughout her entire system—feeling her back against the chair, her feet on the floor. I guide all three of us in doing a quick version of grounding and filling. Mary's presence has now completely returned to her own body. Kelly is visibly more relaxed. I ask Kelly how she is feeling now. She smiles and says, "I cannot believe how much better I feel!"

With this opening, I continue. Using the example of her mom, I ask Kelly to check in and see where the majority of her energy presence is located. She gets very quiet and says, "It's odd; my mom was in front of herself, but I feel more of myself in the *back* of my body and behind me—like I am hiding out a little bit." This is remarkable awareness on her part as a teenager, and I affirm what she is sensing. Her presence *is* pulled back, withdrawn, probably trying to get her space from her mom.

I ask Kelly if she would like to integrate her energetic awareness throughout her entire system by bringing her presence forward. I explain that if she wants to be in her power with her mom, she has to fully inhabit her own body, not hang out somewhere behind it. As she looks puzzled, I ask her awareness questions that help her energy field—her presence—come forward. Such as, "Can you feel the rise and fall of your chest as you breathe?" And, "Does your belly move when you breathe?" She has to move into those parts of her body to get the answers to my questions. As she brings her energy presence more fully into herself, her mom silently, but visibly, relaxes. I nod to her, but keep on going with Kelly.

"Now Kelly, let your awareness expand out a little farther and tell me how your mom's presence feels to you now." Again, silence, but a smile grows on her face. She opens her eyes and looks at me.

"When we began, I hated my mom's presence. It was too much. It was pushing on me all the time. All I could think about was how to get away from her. Now, somehow, it doesn't feel that way. I am not sure how it does feel yet, but I don't hate it anymore."

I ask her how powerful she feels now compared to when we began. This elicits that wonderful grin again.

"I do feel more powerful. Weird—how did you do that?"

I review what *she has done for herself*—awareness returning to the front of her body, grounding and filling, and willingness to learn something new. I have just facilitated her in establishing full body presence. The process has become easy and transparent for her, so she can repeat it at will.

Now we need to return to Kelly's mom. When I ask her how she is doing, she says this is all good, but she is feeling a little worried. She now knows what she was doing wrong, but wonders how can she connect in a way that does not make Kelly want to withdraw. I had noticed earlier that Mary's energy presence had a focused intensity where her daughter was concerned. And while she now knew she could withdraw that intensity at will, there is a fundamental shift she needs to make in the quality of her energy presence in order for the relationship to succeed and be a win-win one. We want healthy connection here, not abdication of power on Mary's part.

I need Kelly's feedback on this next step in order to give it validity. So I ask Kelly to relax fully into her own body and give us feedback as Mary takes this next step. Then I ask Mary to remember a time when she was feeling very happy and relaxed—perhaps after a good massage or out taking a walk. She didn't share what she was thinking, but her whole face relaxed. Her shoulders dropped and a smile came to her face. I asked her to notice how she felt in her body at that moment. She described feeling soft and warm. Her intensity had dispersed. Kelly's face lit up, and she let her mom know how much safer it felt to be with her when she was like that.

I asked Mary to notice what had changed in her body. She said it was as though the molecules had spread out. She felt full, but more diffuse. With her container full, her boundaries felt clearer, yet softer and more flexible. The intensity was gone, and it felt peaceful.

I asked her to notice how connected to Kelly she felt. She smiled again. "I feel *more* connected than before—how could that be?"

I explained that a softer, more diffuse, energy presence is easier to connect with and feels safer. However, it does require that she keep her energy integrated throughout her entire system and stay grounded and full. She understood that, but had never seen its application in an interpersonal way. When she opened her eyes she could still hold that state of full body presence by *drinking in* her daughter, rather than *going out* energetically to meet her. It felt wonderful to Kelly.

But we were not done. Relationship dynamics are made of energy presence, or lack thereof, but also of how we communicate verbally, and I knew this was a part of their relationship that had been rocky. I turned back to Kelly. "So, in the past your m om's presence had gotten too intense when she was asking you questions about your life and friends, right?"

"I feel like she is trying to control me," she blurted out.

Mary looked surprised. That was not her intention, but she could see how it came across that way. I asked Mary what her actual intention is when she is questioning Kelly.

"I really just want to know enough information to ascertain

that Kelly is safe. I want her to learn to stand on her own two feet. I do not want to control her and keep her from learning that."

Now it is Kelly's turn to look surprised.

I ask, "So exactly what information would help you to know that she is safe?"

We go down through a clear list that includes needing to know the people she is with, where they are going, whose parent will be present, and what time she will be home.

"So you aren't going to pry into the details of my social life? Ask me about who likes who, or exactly how the evening went, or anything else?"

"As long as you aren't doing things that are harmful to you, like drugs or drinking, I trust that you can navigate your way through healthy decisions when you are with your friends."

Now Kelly is really surprised. "You'll trust me?"

"As long as I have enough information to be able to reach you quickly in an emergency or if you need help, I will trust you to begin to make your own choices."

I turned to Kelly now. "So Kelly, in order for your mom to have this information that will help her to know you are safe, it is necessary for you to stay in your power and *offer it to her*, so she doesn't have to go into mom-interrogation mode."

Kelly got very quiet. I asked, "Can you do that?" She said she would try.

Mary then agreed to make the exact list of things she needed to know so that Kelly could gather that information for her mom before she asked permission to do something.

This was going to be a stretch for both of them, and they knew it. Kelly had to stay in her full body presence to feel her power and interact with her mom from a more integrated place rather than pulling away and reacting negatively or disrespectfully. Mary had to hold up her end of the bargain by not letting her presence go back to being too intense and invasive. She needed to ask her questions in a clear and grounded way and let Kelly answer them. I agreed to help Mary ascertain what questions were appropriate.

As we finished, they were cautiously optimistic. In the weeks and months that have followed our session, Mary has checked back in daily with *Exploration II* and several times with *Exploration III* for support. She is learning to feel more throughout her body. She holds the fear in her heart in a loving, unconditional way and is learning to discern when she truly needs to be worried and when she can let it go. She called last week to tell me that she had discovered that her gut feelings are a lot more accurate than the fear and worry in her head in terms of whether Kelly is telling her the truth and if she is safe. She is also exploring how to have healthy boundaries around what she allows her daughter to do—how to be connected to her and yet support her healthy independence.

Their relationship is doing much better. It isn't perfect, but now they have the skills to correct things when they start to go astray. When she can stay in her full body presence, which enables her to stand in her power, Kelly's interactions with her mom are much more productive and respectful. Naturally, there have been setbacks. Kelly has made mistakes like all teenagers. When things go awry they can return to that state more quickly—often within minutes or hours. Now they are able to sit together, check in with how present they are, and communicate from a more grounded, steady place.

~

Specific Suggestions

If you want to work with relationship issues, particularly complex or longstanding issues that may have multiple layers, the third segment of *Exploration III* is designed for you. It includes awareness questions and suggestions that can help you tune in and move in a healing direction.

The following suggestions may also be valuable:

1. To discover what your energy presence is like in a particular relationship, listen to *Exploration I* as you bring that person to mind, as though they are sitting across from you.

2. Notice where in your body you have most sensation and where you have numbness. Notice if you are withdrawing or leaning into the other person energetically. Notice if any part of you opens up or closes off as you imagine being in this person's presence. For instance, when someone is falling in love they tend to feel a sense of opening up in the presence of their beloved. If someone is struggling in a relationship, they often feel parts of themselves wanting to close up or to protect themselves in the presence of the other person.

3. Use *Exploration II and III*: ground, fill up, and cradle, with unconditional love, the parts of yourself that you feel locked out of or not present in—where you have a

disrupted body presence. Allow your energy field to expand into those areas, challenging any limiting beliefs you may have about living in those parts of your body.

For instance, if you are a teenager, you may feel as though you have to retreat or fight with your parents. Try being solidly grounded with full body presence as you negotiate for what works for all of you.

Being grounded with full body presence when you are around your teenager, it is easier as a parent to feel what is right in any given moment, and what is 'off'. Trust your gut on this. Don't insist that your children be like everyone else, but also don't relinquish your power to them when something feels 'off'. It is your responsibility to make sure your children are guided safely through their teenage years. Don't walk away energetically in order to keep the peace. Doing so creates temporary harmony, but you'll pay for it in the long run. Meet your children where they are and call on them to be responsible human beings. Don't expect them to be perfect, and don't 'let them off the hook' when they need to take responsibility for their actions. This is most easily accomplished by staying as grounded and as full as you can be and working through your own issues so they don't get projected onto your children. Life is too short—enjoy it!

⁓

Integrating this Energy Throughout Your Entire System is an essential element in establishing a full container from which to live and create, using your unique gifts, whatever they may be.

With Julie's fuller, softer container she was experiencing a lot more of the ease and joy—in my treatment room and in her day-to-day life—after each session. Her gifts flowed out more effortlessly as she worked with others.

This principle of *Integration* is also vital to establishing healthy boundaries. Not only does it give you a sense of safety as you interact with others, it also enables your therapeutic presence to feel safe and healing to them.

When Kelly learned to *integrate* her energetic presence fully throughout her body, she was able to show up in her power and resolve issues with her mother, rather than simply fighting about them. When Mary's energy filled out and softened—integrating throughout her entire system—her daughter felt safe again in her presence. Then they could interact with minimal strife. Mary also felt much more connected to her daughter *from inside* her own navigational system—much more likely to accurately sense safety issues. Choosing to *integrate* was the initial and primary action required for transforming their lives. From this point, all the other principles followed easily.

Each of these three people derived different benefits from this principle. Julie gained a clear sense of ease in simply *being* in full body presence. Kelly gained her power, and her ability to navigate in her world, from that sense of integrated power.

Mary gained a deeper sense of connection with her daughter, Kelly, at this critical point in Kelly's development, as well as a clearer sense of her own direction. They all discovered how much easier and more natural it is when life is experienced from inside their bodies.

~

Principle 4

EXPAND Your Perceptual Lens.

Expanding your perceptual lens enables you to see clearly, release expectations and limiting beliefs, and open fully to life.

The following three examples are experiences where the principle in *Expanding Your Perceptual Lens* was the entryway for beginning the healing and integration process. Other principles also are included in these stories, but *Expanding* was the door opener in these three cases. If *Expanding* is the principle that calls to you, or that you have encountered in those around you, read on.

Critical Me

Heather called me for a session when she was three months out of recovery from a knee surgery that had left her non-ambulatory and sedentary for quite a while during the healing process. During that time, she had gained back much of the weight she had lost across the last three years, and she felt overwhelmed by the thought of going back to the gym for her regular workout. She felt heavy and out of control where her body was concerned. She was convinced that she had gotten fat and was being lazy. Her normal full body presence was disrupted on many levels.

After we took enough time to get grounded and full, using *Exploration II*, I checked in with her to see how she was currently feeling inside. She told me she felt sluggish and nauseous. In the next breath, she was muttering about her laziness. I asked her to remember back to how she had felt when she weighed less and was in better shape. She couldn't recall what that felt like at all. She could not get beyond the current feeling of overall sluggishness and the self-judgment that she was somehow at fault for it. It had not yet occurred to her that there could be something else going on in her system that was causing the sluggishness.

Having worked with Heather before, I recognized a familiar pattern, which was the limiting belief that if something was going wrong in her world, she was somehow always at fault. It had to do with her believing she was 'not being good enough'. Her perceptual lens was definitely narrowed and cloudy here.

In previous sessions, we had visited and revisited this particular limiting belief in many areas of her life. Heather had uncovered how her mother's constantly critical attitude toward her as a child had started this belief. In past sessions, Heather had expanded her perceptual lens and realized it wasn't true— that she *was good enough*. In fact, she was an amazing woman, well accomplished in her professional world as well as in the rest of her life.

She had already healed this limiting belief in other areas of her being, so when we discovered the 'not good enough' belief hanging out here in the area of her body image, there was very little resistance to expanding her perceptual lens. She easily opened to the possibility that there was nothing inherently wrong with how she looked, and that she was not somehow at fault for feeling so low on energy. As she held that possibility, the tension from all her self-judgment began to melt. She felt more open and lighter somehow.

From there, she was able to take true responsibility for her health by asking herself what *was* wrong in her biology—in her body—if it weren't about '"being fat and lazy'.

Expanding Heather's perceptual lens broke open a whole cascade of questions and *curiosity*—not judgment—about blood sugar and blood pressure, cholesterol, hormone and thyroid function. We had a detailed conversation with her body. Thus Heather could give her doctor accurate information about how she actually felt, maximizing the possibility that she would get better medical attention. Heather took notes as we went, so that she could take it with her to her next doctor's appointment. She had been dreading her next visit because of the weight gain and not yet getting back to exercising. That all changed as she became a helpful detective about her own health. Heather actually began to look forward to engaging with her physician to solve this mystery, rather than feeling guilty and 'not good enough'.

When we began to discuss the movement that Heather's body could tolerate (we had already ascertained that when she thought about going back to her full workout at the gym it made her shudder), Heather got the image of walking. I suggested that she try a nice, easy walk of 20-30 minutes per day for a couple of weeks.

She immediately hit another limiting belief. If she wasn't going *full out*, it wasn't good enough. A mere walk of 25 minutes a day at a comfortable pace wouldn't do it. She was raised with the words, "Make it count or don't do it at all. Work hard at everything you do. If it's worth doing, its worth doing well." So the only things judged worthwhile in her life were the things she worked really hard at!

Heather quickly realized this was a limiting belief, too, and opened to the possibility that she could see it differently. With that she laughed, realizing that when she thought about walking daily, it felt entirely do-able, unlike returning full out to the gym.

In the meantime, I asked Heather to practice grounding and filling daily, using *Exploration II,* with "her ear to the ground" in her system, asking what was going on, now that she was open to hearing what her body had to tell her. And to do this rather than judging herself and shutting down further communication. She was open, optimistic, and ready to explore when we finished.

~

Specific Suggestions

Expand Your Perceptual Lens was Heather's entryway into her further healing. She had to do it multiple times throughout her session. If you are someone who has a strong inner critic or you second-guess yourself a lot, Segment 2 in *Exploration III,* on releasing limiting beliefs, will be invaluable.

When our inner critic or judgmental parts are driving our bus, they are inevitably using false or outdated limiting beliefs to stay in control and keep us down. Often these limiting beliefs are not even in our conscious awareness. We just know that we are paralyzed or plagued by feeling bad about ourselves for some reason. Heather is actually over the weight limit that feels good to her and is healthy. However, she is a lot better equipped to handle it when she feels okay about herself and is empowered to make changes that are lasting. When Heather's inner critic is haranguing her, she feels helpless, 'not good enough', and paralyzed to do anything about it.

When working on inner critic issues, I advise using each

Exploration daily until the pattern is released and you can clearly think through the issues at hand without an emotional charge.

1. *Exploration I* is vital to discern where in your body the inner critic and its associated pain are headquartered.

2. *Exploration II* is vital for creating a strong, full container to meet and hold the area of pain or judgment in a loving, powerful manner.

3. *Exploration III* is key to releasing those limiting beliefs and moving on in your life with more of you on board.

This process is fairly straightforward, but can take time and repeated effort as the layers of limiting beliefs peel away. Often an outside facilitator is helpful here as a narrowed perceptual lens can look deceptively like the truth if it is longstanding in your life. Remember Heather's layers. Don't let it get you down or stop your process if another layer shows up once you release the one above it. This just shows you are making progress.

As far as I can tell, this process goes on throughout our lives. It gets easier—as you saw it do for Heather—once you have experienced success with releasing some significant layers. Years ago, when Heather was releasing the first few layers of that ingrained limiting belief about 'not being good enough', it took up entire sessions and was accompanied by buckets of tears as she tenaciously worked to release that false belief about herself. As you could see from this session, she was easily able to move through it in minutes. She got it out of the 'driver's seat of her bus', once she recognized it for what it was, and reclaimed her power again. You can do the same thing with practice.

My Anger is Back

One of my clients, John, called and asked if he could come see me. When I asked what was wrong, he admitted that he and his wife had fallen into an old argument, and he had verbally raged at her in a way that was really destructive. On top of that, his back had gone into spasm later that evening.

The next day, as soon as John walked in, I could see that he was in severe pain. In the bodywork session that followed, I used dialoguing skills from CranioSacral therapy, my hands, and my therapeutic presence as healthy resources for his system. As his perceptual lens expanded, he was able to meet his rage and pain in a new, more loving, unconditional way, in order to heal it.

We began the session with my hands gently cradling John's low back and heart, the areas where he felt most disconnected. I could feel the tension, like steel cords, running through the palm of my hand that was on his back. John told me how the health of his lower back has steadily deteriorated over the last seven years and how *angry* he felt about it. "I can't play with my kids. I can't work in my yard. I am afraid of every small sensation— afraid that my back is about to go into yet another excruciating spasm. All I did was take a simple bike ride the last time it went into spasm two weeks ago. I feel fragile and I *hate* feeling fragile."

I felt the intensity of his dilemma as he described it. His back got tighter under my hand as he talked. He had a severe disruption in his full body presence, and it was manifesting right under my hands. It was clear to me that John could not see a way out of this cycle of injury, diminished capacity, and despair. I could sense his limited vision of himself—rigid, old age unfolding before him at the age of 49. His narrowed perceptual lens had blinded John to the inner resources that could assist him in healing. At that moment, he was unaware that such resources even existed. So his first step was to *expand* his perceptual lens so that he could see a new possibility for himself. My role then became one of helping him find his deeper wisdom and meet the parts of himself that he was locked out of in order for him to reclaim his full body presence and heal.

As we began, he allowed his awareness to drop into his lower back, describing what he noticed. His breathe slowed and deepened as he sank in there.

"What strikes you first?" I asked gently. "Don't edit anything or think it through for validity—just say what hits you first."

"It feels like a huge log. A tree trunk without the roots or branches."

I concurred. His lower back felt immovable, large, and hard, not like normal, healthy back tissue. His heart, under my other hand, had an echo of hardness as well.

"How long has it been like this?" I asked gently.

I felt the hardness soften as he answered, "I don't know, but I suddenly feel a very deep sadness as I let myself connect with your hands." His perceptual lens was starting to expand.

Again, I concurred, because I was registering the sadness as it left him. I saw a small boy in my mind's eye, and moments later, John said to me, "I feel about four years old."

The hardness softened even more as he described a bleak world, feeling alone, riding in a car, feeling terrified of his father's rages, and his mother's inability to protect him. I asked John how the little boy coped with all of that.

"I did what I watched my father do. I got angry and stayed angry all the time, to create a protective shield around myself." He added, "I excelled in school so that I knew a lot, but I kept my anger out in front of me *all the time*. I won in all my debates. I could lacerate my enemies verbally."

I asked John how that related to the tree trunk in his back. He was quiet for a few moments. Then he replied, "In order to stay angry all the time, my system has to stay on red alert, and that little boy in my lower back is *still* on red alert."

I asked him if he needed to be on red alert any longer. He got quiet, and I felt his back start to soften. His perceptual lens was expanding even further as he chuckled, and I felt his back relax several more layers. He realized he'd unnecessarily carried that little boy in his hardened, rigid lower back all these years.

I asked John if there is anywhere else that little boy would rather be, and he replied quickly, "He wants to be held, in my heart."

I felt the rest of his back soften as the little boy—his vulnerability—moved in his mind's eye to his heart. I could also feel his heart soften and fill under my hand, as the little boy curled up safely there.

Then a strange sensation began. I felt a numb, pins-and-needles sensation coming through my hand that was still holding his lower back. It went on for about four minutes. Then it passed, as though his back was letting go of the residual numbness and rigidity. At that point, he had fully returned to his lower back, and it was no longer in pain. It felt soft and relaxed. His heart felt full, with a good flow of energy moving through it. His anger no longer owned him. Having *expanded* his perceptual lens, he was able to utilize his energetic awareness to *integrate* his presence throughout his entire system.

John shared how exhausted he felt in the aftermath of holding on this tightly for so long. Then his breath deepened, and he went into a quiet relaxed state as we finished the session.

His full body presence was palpable. His anger had dissolved.

When John stood up, his back felt softer. I suggested that the next time he felt a twinge of sensation in his back, he greet it with curiosity rather than anger and frustration. Then ask that sensation what it was trying to tell him. He agreed that he would try to do that and seemed much more at peace with his body as we closed.

This example shows how the skills taught in this book and on the audio are utilized in a hands-on bodywork session. John could have worked on his own with holding his lower back in his healing-energy hands. It may have taken him longer to achieve the integration we reached in the session together. When the part of yourself that you want to re-integrate involves a highly charged, longstanding issue, like John's anger, one resource that is often vital is another human being who is grounded and holding a therapeutic presence. That therapeutic presence supports you in exploring a vulnerable, scary place without being overwhelmed by it.

As the facilitator of his healing process, my most important role was to stay grounded, with full body presence, so that I could provide the cushion of energy that he needed to move through this long-standing problem. Throughout the session I checked in, again and again, to make sure that I was as present as I could be for his healing process to unfold.

Also, remember how John brought his energetic awareness to his lower back? When, as a client, you add *your* energetic awareness to the alchemy of your healing sessions, the outcome is exponentially greater. So, stay present each time you receive a healing session and use the skills you have learned here to get more out of every treatment you receive.

~

Specific Suggestions

The first step for John was to *expand his perceptual lens* around the pain in his back—energetically moving from seeing himself as a victim of back pain to experiencing and releasing the sadness and anger associated with it. Your entry point may differ. If you are struggling to integrate really strong emotions and sensations and finding that they tend to take over in your life, or 'drive your bus' right off the cliff, which in turn causes your relationships with others to suffer, the following information will be helpful:

1. First you have to recognize and own that *you have* whatever the emotion is and not project it out onto someone else in your world. Oftentimes, when we have strong emotions that feel unacceptable to us, we feel bad about them deep inside. So we justify why they are there, and why we have a right to dump them on those in our lives. So the first step is to recognize and take responsibility for your feelings, your emotions.

2. Notice where the emotion anchors in your body. Where is the root of your anger or the core of your fear in your body?

3. Use *Exploration III* to hold this place and work with the pain, or whatever is under the emotion, until it is integrated. Remember with a long-standing emotional pattern like John exhibited, you may need to do this in

layers. It is greatly aided by finding a well-trained hands-on therapist to provide a therapeutic presence for you to do this.

New Ways of Perceiving a Self-Centered Friend

Trish is a wonderful, vivacious woman, full of life, caring, and energy. She is also self-centered in a way that does not take into account many of her time commitments, or others around her. Years ago, when we would pick her up to go to a party together, she would invariably be anywhere from 20 to 45 minutes late. Those of us waiting for her would get frustrated. Then angry. Then resigned, to what we saw as her lack of thoughtfulness. Sometimes we left her. It never changed, no matter how much we complained. She would just laugh nervously and brush it off, saying that she was sorry and she would be on time the next time.

I resolved this issue with her by expanding my own perceptual lens. I had to recognize that her lateness was *her* issue and that I had enough power and presence to not be at the mercy of it. I still love her as a friend, but I recognize that she has this issue and *it has nothing to do with me*. So I no longer ride to events with her. I see her at the event, in her own time. If she misses the beginning, so be it—it's not my issue. I don't ask her to bring the appetizers to a shared meal. I ask her to bring one of her delicious desserts. I go to see her at her own home. Although she is usually not ready, we can connect and talk at her house, without her being ready.

So I have expanded my perceptual lens to see her clearly for who she is, *not who I want her to be only to feel constantly disappointed*. I love her for who she is, for her loyalty as a friend, and her caring heart. And, recognizing her limitations, I don't expect her to act like someone she is not. I choose to expand my lens to see how she actually operates in the world so I can realistically meet her and enjoy her company. I no longer have a narrow vision of her as rude or inconsiderate.

Please notice that I am *not* talking about how to make my friend change. I simply widened *my* perceptual lens. There are examples of situations where I have helped the person who is out of sync with their world to establish a full body presence and reconnect with the world because it is important to them— not to make me or anyone else happy. Although these kinds of changes probably will make others happy, you simply cannot be making the change solely to make someone else happy at your own expense.

We get into such trouble with our fellow humans when we expect them to act as we would act and then take it as a personal affront if they don't. Instead of viewing others with expectations and judgment, we can *expand* our perceptual lens. Think about limiting beliefs you may have been raised with around such issues as lateness, affection, being polite versus telling the truth, etc. Notice what you assume about the other person when they don't act as you expect them to. Can you expand your perceptual lens and include a world where being on time is different from the way you were raised? Can you include this other person's reality and walk in their shoes? If you are the person who is chronically late, can you walk in the shoes of the person you are keeping waiting?

Exploration III, Segment 2, deals specifically with expanding your perceptual lens, so if this is an issue for you, use that resource. Remember, you may have to use it repeatedly if it is a longstanding or deeply ingrained belief that you hold.

During the period of my life when I was the mother of two young children, I was chronically late. I am still more relaxed about time than my husband. Also, having lived in several cultures, experiencing how differently people in southern Europe or on an Indian reservation treat time, has given me a more expanded lens on time. It doesn't mean I enjoy being kept waiting. It *does* mean I don't lose my full body presence. And I am energetically aware of how the waiting is affecting me versus unconsciously being depleted by it (which I would have been at one point in my life).

~

Specific Suggestions

If you have a friend or colleague like Trish who cannot see beyond themselves in certain areas of their lives, if you have a self-centered family member, someone that you have put on a pedestal, or someone you have written off due to unmet expectations, the following instructions may be valuable:

1. Make the choice to expand you perceptual lens. It is important to be able to see the person for who he or she *actually is* rather than whom you *want* him or her to be, or expect them to be. This takes the charge out of the issue and helps you decide what to do about your unmet expectations in a much more clear-headed manner.

2. To get beyond your disappointment, anger, or frustration, you may want to begin by asking yourself what you are expecting from someone that they are not giving you. Initially, this expectation may be completely

outside of your conscious awareness. However, if you ask yourself and sit with it for a short while, it will often come to you. Sometimes someone close to you can help you with this if they have heard you complain about this person.

3. The next question to ask is how you are interpreting their inability to do what you want, or expect them to do, such as in these situations:

- Someone who is consistently late for commitments

- Someone who misinterprets your requests and does something differently than what you wanted or asked for

- Someone who does not offer to help in a situation in which you would have definitely offered to help out

- Someone who remains silent when you think they should have spoken up or speaks up when you think silence is needed

- Someone who does not see you or your needs clearly, consistently attributing things to you, that are not true

- Someone you think should be perfect because they know so much more than you do—how could they make a mistake?

4. What do you decide about *them* and about *yourself* from their behavior? (This could range from judging them as bad or inferior or cowardly to judging yourself as not good enough, or that they don't care enough about you to do what you want.)

5. How could you see this differently? How else could you interpret their words or actions? Really expand your perceptual lens on how you are seeing this event or situation . . . what else could they have meant by their actions? Imagine the opposite of what you originally thought—what would that story sound like? Can you be open to the possibility that the truth lies somewhere in between?

6. When you have expanded your lens sufficiently, you can often start to see this person more accurately—*as they are*—rather than what you judge them to be. You will know this is the case when you no longer feel a charge about what you think of them. For instance, if I forget and ask Trish to bring the appetizer, and she shows up 45 minutes late, I don't get angry with her. I am frustrated with the situation. Mostly, I am frustrated with myself for forgetting this is who she is. As my teenaged son would say, "Oops, my bad."

7. Utilize *Exploration III* through all three segments to clear the whole range of issues, from expanding your awareness to healing limiting beliefs to feeling deeper ease in your relationships.

∽

Expanding Your Perceptual Lens is an essential element in healing and standing in your power and not being pulled around by external influences.

The inner screen of our navigational system is clearer and more accurate when our perceptual lens *expands*. This is also the principle which teaches us to gather new information when we need to resolve an issue in our lives. Finding a book, embracing a new point of view by listening to someone else's perspective, learning about other cultures and religions are all helpful in expanding your perceptual lens.

Heather's entire health issue shifted when she expanded her perceptual lens to see herself in a different light. John's physical healing was able to unfold once his perceptual lens expanded around his back pain—cracking open the door to *feeling* nourishing sensation, *integrating* it throughout his system, and learning to *choose* healthier resources in the future. I gained a deeper sense of connection with my wonderful friend when I expanded my perceptual lens to see her more accurately and release my limiting beliefs about time.

As you can see in these examples, once the door was open, all the other principles of *feeling, choosing, trusting*, and *integrating* follow easily. Expanding your perceptual lens can initiate the establishment of full body presence, where you can listen to your internal landscape and operate from your navigational system rather than from fear and limiting beliefs.

∽

Principle 5

CHOOSE nourishing resources
moment to moment

*Choosing moment to moment to connect to healthy
resources requires commitment, courage, and kindness,
and provides you with a steady foundation
and a deep sense of inner peace.*

The following two examples are experiences where the principle of *Choosing Nourishing Resources Moment to Moment* was the entryway for beginning the healing and transformation process. Other principles also are included in these stories, but Principle 5—Choosing was the door opener in these two cases. If this principle is the one that calls to you, or that you have encountered in those around you, read on.

Wise Choice for Third Marriage

Deborah is now in her early 40's, happily married with three children. But this was not always the case. As a younger woman, Deborah married her first husband because she thought she should. All her friends were married, and her mother and grandmother were both married by age 21. It was what she was supposed to do. She made the choice from the 'ought to' in her head rather than from her inner wisdom. She had no modeling for making healthy choices from a full body presence. Without energetic awareness, she had no way of contacting her inner wisdom.

Within a few years it became obvious that her relationship was ending, as they both wanted very different things. She had no skills—no internal resources—to resolve those differences. She divorced her husband and married again very quickly in order to remedy the mistake she felt she had made in ending her marriage. No one in her family had ever divorced, and her shame felt overwhelming. To get away from it, she married a man she didn't really even have feelings for but who *looked* like the kind of man she should marry. The relationship became abusive and quickly proved to be an unhealthy connection, further disrupting her body presence. Somehow she sensed this and left within the year.

With two marriages in ruins, Deborah finally stopped running from herself. She chose to begin to nurture herself by learning the skills taught in *Exploration I* of how to feel her internal landscape and listen to her own inner wisdom. As she learned to ground and fill, healing her disrupted body presence, it furthered her ability to discern more healthy resources. Using *Exploration III*, she learned to meet and gently, lovingly hold the pain in her heart and the shame in her belly. And over time, it dissolved and healed. She relaxed and gave herself permission to live by her own inner timing, rather than rushing to do what others thought was correct. This enabled her to discern what resources were truly healthy for her at that point in her life and to choose them consistently.

When Deborah met her current husband, she did not act too quickly, as she had previously done. She made a strong commitment to herself to choose healthy resources. She took the time to let herself fully explore what she wanted. She was feeling a growing sense of strength and worthiness for the first time in her life as her full body presence developed. When she had the courage to make the decision to remarry, it was with a clarity, steadiness, and sense of inner peace she had never felt before.

Deborah now knows what she wants and practices asking for it in her relationship. She is willing to negotiate differences with her husband, and her current marriage is a healthy, fulfilling one. Deborah has enough sense of herself internally to navigate through it without losing her integrity. She has flourished creatively as well. So everyone is a winner in this equation—Deborah, her husband, their children, and her creative life. She continues to choose nourishing resources moment to moment—keeping her container full and her navigational system intact.

⌇

Specific Suggestions

Choosing Nourishing Resources Moment to Moment was the first step for Deborah. If you have had experiences of making unhealthy choices based on fear, shame, or guilt, rather than healthy choices from your deep inner wisdom, then read on. These suggestions will also be valuable if you find that you make good choices most of the time, but then find yourself racked with fear, shame, or guilt that you did it incorrectly.

1. A key for moving beyond fear, shame, or guilt is to change our internal resonance. When we are dominated by fear, shame, or guilt, our systems reverberate dissonantly with the emotions that are controlling us. We can often feel this tension when we slow down and tune in. On the other hand, when we are connected to healthy resources and energetically full, our resonance is deep, and it feels good. This resonance is the signature of full body presence. It is a

state of being that is life-giving. It has a hum, or a vibration, to it that sustains us over time. This resonance is also a signal that we have the container to be able to hold and heal those painful places inside where fear, shame, or guilt dwell. What follows will help you shift your resonance in a healthier direction.

2. Start with *Exploration II, Grounding and Filling*, to provide a full container to operate from. When we are not feeling really full and present, it is easy to let fear sway our lives. If we are grounded with full body presence, we naturally register what we feel inspired to do versus what we are afraid may happen.

3. Once you have identified where the pain and disconnect is anchored within your body, utilize *Exploration III* to hold and love this place unconditionally. Do so until it resolves and integrates so that you can love all of you.

4. Regular practice of all of the *Explorations* is important until it is second nature to check inside yourself and keep refilling. Then your life choices are more informed by your inner wisdom—with input from your navigational system—and in your own time. Know that emotions such as fear, shame, and guilt can be powerful, hidden instigators of repeated self-destructive actions in our lives. Be kind and gentle with yourself, and committed to finding and healing the places inside where these emotions are trapped. The energy payoff for healing these places can be immense.

5. Also, please work with the second and third segments of *Exploration III*. They are designed to help you trace and heal any limiting beliefs entwined with fear, guilt, or shame. This will support you in healing your relationships with yourself and others that are affected negatively by these beliefs and emotions. It also provides you with a steady foundation.

I Don't Know What I Want from My Husband

(Note to reader: If you are experiencing challenges in your most intimate relationship, carefully read this account. Following the story, specific suggestions are listed which can help those who suspect that they may be accommodating those in their world rather than really showing up and getting their needs met. There is also a section of specific suggestions for healing relationships.)

Jodi and Philip have been consciously working to improve their marriage for years. They are at a very pivotal point. It is a point that happens for all couples somewhere in the journey of their relationships. It is the time when fundamental change has to happen for one or both partners if the relationship is going to continue to grow and flourish.

What I have found is that the energy skills taught here immeasurably support and deepen that level of fundamental change as well as the work they are doing elsewhere in their world, be it couples or individual therapy, or some other form of bodywork or healing.

The following happened while they were in my office for an appointment together. We usually talk initially, and then they each take turns getting on the treatment table for a hands-on CranioSacral session in which the other person helps out. This account is from Jodi's half of the session as she describes moving across the threshold into their relationship in a deeper way.

Jodi starts by telling me the hard realizations she had recently in a couple's therapy session.

> I recognized that I am a classic accommodator to everyone else's needs. I rarely know what I really want deep down. I say "yes" in far too many circumstances when I want to say "no". I give people what they want, so they'll leave me alone. I feel 'invisible' in my life in many ways. I am realizing now that I really was invisible as a child. My alcoholic father never really saw me at all. He was too wrapped up in his own pain. My mother was an accommodator as well, ambivalent about having children probably because of my dad's alcoholism. All three of us felt her ambivalence at some level, but me especially.
>
> I have recently become aware of how I overcompensate for that feeling of invisibility by being very funny, very entertaining, and 'out there.' I am excellent at sensing what is going on with others, to the detriment of knowing myself.

Jodi is seeing herself accurately here. At times her presence *is* scattered and hard to connect with. In certain moments when we are together, we are absolutely in sync, and the next moment she is gone. Jodi continues,

> I am just realizing that I have serious difficulty knowing what I really want in my marriage. Philip wants to connect more deeply with me. He's done his own work of backing off and

not judging and badgering me. And you know how I have worked to open up to him—all these years of therapy and bodywork to resolve my childhood traumas. Now the issue is really coming to a head in our marriage. I feel stuck. I can see what I am doing; I just don't know how to move through this. I don't know how to make healthy choices for myself.

The process of being in relationships that nourish everyone requires courage, skill, and commitment; and it is well worth the work involved. In fact, it is what makes life full and juicy rather than dry and unhappy. The latest brain research shows that when love and compassion are present, the brain lights up and operates to its fullest capacity. We truly are meant to live from a deep sense of interconnectedness with our world, and our relationships are a huge part of that process.

Whether we are talking about your beloved mate, your child, your best friend, your parent, your boss, or a colleague, the principles of a healthy relationship all build from the same foundation. This is the steady foundation that full body presence provides and that enables you to choose what is life giving and say "no" to what is life-taking *for you*. Within that knowing of yourself and your needs, there are many twists and turns in the path to healthy enjoyable relationships, but they all start with full presence.

Let's return to Jodi and Philip in my office. She has just shared that insightful awareness about her life-long pattern— her default stance—of accommodating others, and she is relaxing on the treatment table. My hands are supporting her spine. Philip asks her where she would like to have his hands— in other words, what she wants from him in this session. She tells him, "Oh, hold anywhere; it doesn't matter."

It strikes me in that moment that she does not know how to make contact with her deep inner knowing and choose what she truly wants—what would be life-enhancing for her. I also sense that she is not in her bones, the deep recesses of who she is. I can sense that she is in the more superficial parts of her body, but not it's most intimate, inner chambers. She doesn't have her full body presence. This is reflected in the lack of energetic awareness and her response to Philip.

I ask her to notice what she feels or doesn't feel deep inside her body, in her bones. She is quiet for a moment. She admits she cannot feel that part of herself. Gently guiding her to drop her awareness back in her body, into the part in contact with the treatment table, I use my relaxed flat hand on her spine to help her orient around a warm, physical sensation. Continuing to help her drop in, I ask, "What does the table feel like where your spine is touching it?" and then, "Can you feel the back of your head on the table?" and then, "What do your feet feel like in Philip's hands?" My questions are designed to help her feel more of her internal landscape.

I feel her slowly settling deeper into her body, and as she does so, she spontaneously comes out with what she really wants from Philip. "I would like your hands on my heels, Philip, not the tops of my feet. Yes, that feels much better. Thank you." And later in the session when Philip tries to move too soon for her, she speaks up immediately and says, "Please stay there longer. Your hands there feel wonderfully settling."

Previously she was *not even registering* what she really wanted deep inside—what her deepest needs were. Now, she is choosing clearly and asking for what she wants without even thinking about it. She finally *knows* what she wants! So as the session unfolded, she began to feel not only more of her spine, she began to feel the whole back of her body more. She felt palpably more settled and grounded. Jodi and Philip are both very pleased as we finish up, and she is fully present in her body.

None of her superficial chatter and jokes were there to keep intimacy at a distance. Jodi and Philip nuzzle each other, and I can feel a distinct difference in their connection level from when we began. She is now much easier inside, much more deeply at home. Her needs and desires are not a mystery anymore. She can feel what she needs. She is making healthy choices for herself. He can feel it. And it is delicious.

On their next visit, when I ask Philip how it is to have her knowing and choosing what she wants, and speaking up now, he tells me he is delighted. Then he grins and adds, "Well, it can be momentarily rough as I am getting called on something that isn't working for her, but honestly, I love it. I have a wife who is real. I know where she stands. I can trust her presence in our relationship much more now. I have always known she was in there somewhere; I just couldn't figure out how to get her to come out!" Jodi's grin in response is genuine and straight from her heart (and bones!).

～

Specific Suggestions

If you *suspect* you are an accommodator, *Choosing Nourishing Resources Moment to Moment,* is probably your prime challenge. The following list of questions to ask yourself may be valuable:

1. Do I try to please and nurture everyone else *before* myself?

2. Do I sometimes, or often, have difficulty even knowing what I need, what would feed and nourish me?

3. Do I find myself running around 'out there' in my world, overdoing with little rest time for myself?

4. Is my self-care, when I do it, last on the list behind my significant other, my children, my pets, etc.?

5. Do I have a limiting belief(s) that says that taking care of myself is being selfish?

The strength of someone with this 'accommodator' default stance is that they are often accurate readers of what is going on with their loved ones. They may have spent their lives cultivating the skill of listening to the needs of others. So, they are often good in anticipating the needs of those they love the most. This, of course, must be balanced by *choosing* to meet their own needs by knowing how to drop deep inside, listen to their own inner landscape, and access their own navigational system.

So, if you answered, "yes" to three or more of the questions above, or you know that you have a similar pattern but it looks different on the surface, then the following suggestions are for you.

For an accommodator, it is extra important that you learn to slow down and listen to *your* deep inner places. This includes:

1. Practice with *Exploration I, Opening Awareness*, and *Exploration II, Grounding and Filling*, regularly (daily for a while).

2. Journal your inner experiences, sensations, emotions, and especially any limiting beliefs that show up.

3. Notice what areas of your body you are not living in, or that have pain or numbness when you ask yourself the questions about accommodating to other people. Many times it will be your bones or some part of you deep inside. Often when you approach such an area, a limiting belief will come up that tries to tell you "it is not safe to rest back in yourself" or that you "have to be on 'red alert', scanning the environment all the time in order to know that you are okay." It may try to tell you something about not letting who you truly are inside be seen by the world—"it's more safe to stay invisible". Your particular limiting beliefs and messages may be slightly different. Listen to yourself here—recognize what these limiting beliefs are trying to convince you of so you can expand beyond them.

4. Make sure that you are grounded and full. Use *Exploration III* for support and to hold this place you feel locked out of, or that you don't yet fully inhabit. Hold it and love it, as completely as you can at this time.

5. Being gentle with this process. As you come to completion, notice in particular what you are feeling inside. Any increased clarity about your needs, what internal itch needs to be scratched, or what yearning may be bubbling up?

6. Repeat this *Exploration* as many times as needed to release and integrate all the layers.

Deepening Your Interpersonal Dynamics

If you are working to make healthy choices around relationships and you find yourself mired in interpersonal dynamics that drain you, read on.

Take a moment now and bring to mind a relationship in your life. Using the skills from *Exploration I, Opening Awareness*, take an internal reading on where you are in respect to this relationship. Receive whatever information your body may have for you. Be as open as is possible at this time.

Sometimes our bodies give us messages that we don't want to hear, so we push them away. Can you sense any level of shielding yourself from this person? Many years ago, I was with my intimate other. I discovered that when I stood across from him I had a very subtle sense of shielding my heart from him. In my normal waking state of consciousness, I would never have said I felt that way about him, but as I stood there, my heart informed me that there were trust issues there that I needed to address.

Notice whether you have any limiting beliefs or painful phrases surfacing in your consciousness as you open to whatever awareness is there for you. Is this familiar, or is this a surprise? Is there a memory attached to it? If so, where do you feel *that* in your body?

The next step is to work with the skills from *Exploration II*. Take time to get grounded and fill up. If the relationship you are exploring right now is a life-giving one, you will feel better and better as you fill up. And you will have more of yourself to share with this other person. The other person will probably experience you as more present, more available, and more joyful in the relationship. These skills are fabulous relationship enhancers, creating the optimal circumstances for ecstatic spiritual experiences and deep intimacy. The simplest of interactions can become rich and delicious. Sometimes when I am feeling full and in the present moment, a heartfelt smile from someone I don't even know can warm me to my bones.

But what about when you are emotionally hooked by what is going on in the relationship and you feel tension, contraction, pain, numbness, fear, or shame in the presence of this other person? This is the richest area of learning for us as human beings, but it is the hardest to *want* to work with. In successfully traversing and healing this kind of dynamic, we can grow immensely, opening up whole new worlds of opportunity. So, how do we do this?

Use *Exploration III*. All three segments are designed to work together to lead you through each of the steps that can support you in healing the layers of pain and disconnection. It happens in your own time, in a way you can integrate. Sometimes healing comes quickly in a rush of energy. At other times, it slowly moves in, and one day you realize you are not struggling anymore.

Sometimes it looks like the realization you need to change the nature of the relationship. An example of this might be creating more distance from someone who refuses to interact in respectful, non-abusive ways. It might look like more clearly delineating the boundaries with someone who has trouble with boundaries, if it is someone with which you want to stay in relationship. For example, setting clear house rules with a teenager who needs to understand how the world works in terms of how they treat others.

In the process of working with *Exploration III* with your relationships, often you will discover a part of your body you are locked out of for some reason. This could be your heart, your voice, your pelvis, or your bones.

~

Choosing Nourishing Resources Moment to Moment was an important first step for Deborah, as well as Jodi.

The other principles followed easily. What was important for Deborah was to *choose* to slow down and explore her internal landscape. Having made that choice, she was able to integrate energy throughout her entire system, establishing a full body presence. This gave her a sense of steadiness and inner peace. She was then able to make healthy choices on a moment to moment basis.

Jodi made a commitment to connect more deeply with her internal landscape, giving her the courage to reclaim deeper parts of herself. She was then able to *choose* to ask for what she needed and wanted in a given moment. Jodi and Philip's choice to commit more deeply to their relationship exemplified the patience and kindness that is necessary to this process of healing. *Choosing* healthy resources is an essential component to experiencing full body presence.

~

I hope that you have enjoyed the case histories and anecdotal stories contained in this chapter. These personal accounts demonstrate the power and effectiveness of working with the Five Principles of *Trusting, Feeling, Integrating, Expanding,* and *Choosing* in the process of establishing full body presence. I am always touched by the courage and commitment of those willing to turn their awareness inward, explore their internal landscape, and experience full body presence.

Make a commitment to explore you.
The results are life giving and transforming.

Chapter Nine

~

Guidelines for Living and Working with Others:

The Gift of Your Presence

I f you are regularly working with the *Five Principles* and the *Explorations* you will begin to notice a change in yourself; a change for the better—more energy, more self-awareness, more strength and confidence to meet life on your own terms. You have learned that caring for yourself and treating yourself with respect gives you more ease and resilience in the world. You don't tire as easily, and you don't fear life's demands. You are able to be present to the demands of others without feeling overwhelmed or exhausted. You know how to say "no" when appropriate You know how to turn inward, to nourish yourself and maintain your vitality. You understand that *you* are part of the unconditional sea of energy that surrounds us.

Now I want to explore how you can give the gift of your presence, which is what you now have to offer, to one degree or another, to those in your world. Your full body presence matters. And the gift of your presence is most potent when you are grounded, connected, and fully present in the face of whatever comes up. It involves being compassionate without taking on others' pain. It means maintaining your own healthy boundaries without losing your energy to others in your desire to help. Simply put, your energetic *presence* has a healing effect on others. You are learning how to be in touch with and nurturing of yourself, so that your presence can catalyze and nurture the healing process of others.

Developing the ability to be a strong therapeutic presence is one of the greatest gifts you can give yourself and those around you. It connects you more deeply with your world in a way that opens you fully to life. Your confidence in yourself as a healing presence will increase as you practice the skills taught in this book, as you learn to embody them more and more in your daily life.

Professional caregivers—bodyworkers, counselors, ministers, healthcare practitioners, life coaches, and teachers—are not the only ones who need to nurture themselves and maintain healthy boundaries. All of us are caregivers of one another on some level. We care for our partners, our parents, and our children. We care for our employees or our bosses. We are there for our friends. We volunteer at hospitals, food kitchens, and homeless shelters. All of us can benefit from the skills that professional caregivers learn.

What I would like to leave you with is a set of practical guidelines for serving as a healing presence for others. It is adapted from guidelines I developed for professional healthcare practitioners. You will see the principles for full body presence woven throughout. Following these precepts will keep you from falling into old patterns and increase the steadiness and strength of your own healing presence.

Consider the following BEFORE you engage with someone in your life who needs your caring presence, whether it's your child or your next-door neighbor or a client:

Take Care of You

Nurture the conviction that you deserve to take care of yourself. This is not only good for those you care for—it is an essential part of your birthright as a human being. 'Put your own oxygen mask on first' so there will be someone to help those in need around you. Changing your attitude to reflect this self-respect can make all the difference in the world.

Check In

Take a reading of where you are on the inside. Take a moment to check out your body's internal landscape so you'll know if you're energetically full or depleted. If your energy is low, take enough time to ground and fill yourself. This is an excellent thing to do first thing in the morning so you can plan your day accordingly.

Connect and Fill

Connect to healthy resources in your life—make it a habit. Learn what fills and nourishes you so you can engage others with a full, steady sense of presence. This might involve feeling your feet on the ground, the steadiness of the earth, and the nourishing energy it can provide. It might simply mean taking a few slow, nurturing breaths. Or it might mean taking the time to call on Spirit or summon the image of a special mentor or teacher.

Clearly Set Your Intention

Articulate to yourself what it is you hope to accomplish. For instance, "I want to be present to my son Lenny's fear about football tryouts, and to know where to facilitate his confidence in whatever ways I can." This does not mean having an agenda for the person. It does mean knowing clearly where your boundaries are in terms of what you are willing to do.

Affirm Your Current Realities

"I am here today, to hold this space for Lenny, to the degree that I can, even though I am tired (or preoccupied, or late for work, or Lenny is being sullen)." Accept the realities of your current circumstances rather than denying them. This enables you to better work with these limitations rather than being tripped up by them.

You are not Alone

Remind yourself that you are not the only resource for those you want to help. Everyone has a variety of friends or counselors and unseen inner and outer support. You are not solely responsible for this person's process. We all live in this sea of energy—trust it for them as well, even if they cannot feel it right now. Your trust gives you a steadier presence, which can help them remember and connect with their support more easily.

Consider the following WHILE you are with the person you want to help:

Hold a Space of Compassion and Acceptance

A caring, non-judgmental attitude that meets others where they are is vital to healing. To do this more easily, bring your full body presence, grounded and full, to the situation. Silently repeating a simple prayer, quotation, or poem that inspires your compassion and acceptance is one of many ways you can set your intention and deepen your sense of caring. Such as the Buddhist prayer:

> *May you be happy.*
> *May you be peaceful.*
> *May you be healthy.*

One of my other favorites is the Serenity Prayer used so widely in 12-step programs.

> *God grant me the serenity to accept the things I cannot change,*
> *The courage to change the things I can,*
> *And the wisdom to know the difference.*

The paradox of this attitude is that while it may seem on the surface to be one in which nothing gets done, in actuality, when we adopt an attitude of compassion and acceptance, it opens the door to limitless possibilities. The walls of self-judgment come down in the presence of true acceptance and compassion.

Self-love can then well up in ways not previously known. And it is in the energy presence of love that true healing can occur.

Establish Healthy Boundaries

Be a container large enough for the experiences you encounter. Therapeutic presence communicates steadiness and clarity through your body language. This presence says that you welcome and can handle memories, feelings, or experiences that may arise. If you need to say "no" to something, you do. This is what healthy boundaries are about. Until you can say "no," it is difficult to convey a wholehearted "yes" to what is being asked of you.

Establish and maintain clear boundaries. Be present in your own body, and know what your internal landscape feels like. This kind of intimate self-knowledge tells you where your body stops and the other person begins. Learn to clearly differentiate your sensations and emotions from those of the person you are with. Stay within your own body, without energetically leaning into the other person in order to help; it feels a lot safer and more comfortable to them as well.

Another paradox arises here. Most of us naturally do lean into whomever we are trying to help. But what feels safest to someone in need is a caregiver with full body presence that is wide, diffuse, and not highly focused on them. The steadiness of the caregiver's grounded presence, combined with a wide, non-invasive energy field and touch is what facilitates healing most effectively. Then the system of the person in need can come forward and inform you of what it needs in order to heal. This is a basic CranioSacral principle that applies everywhere else in life as well.

Be aware when your own emotional issues are being triggered, and know what to do about them. Signs of this might include feeling uncomfortable, needing the person you're with to respond in a certain way (i.e., to be relaxed and comfortable) or see you in a certain way (i.e., as the 'all-knowing person' who is helping them). This would be a sign of a hidden agenda on your part. Notice when you are trying to control the outcomes or needing to talk when silence would be golden.

If you discover your own emotional issues coming to the surface in response to the situation you are in, silently recognize them, own them, and, as soon as is appropriate, address them in some way. This could be using *Exploration III* or seeing a therapist or mentor to work them out.

If you are touching the person you are helping, whether casually (i.e., a supportive hand on their shoulder or perhaps holding their hand) or using some form of therapeutic technique, listen to what your body, hands, and intuition tell you. As you know by now, our bodies provide us with a magnificent navigational system. As we regain the ability to be more fully in our bodies, we naturally develop our own unique set of receptors that inform us about others' physical, emotional, and spiritual states. Learning to read the signals from this rich navigational system might include: listening to your gut feeling about whether your time together is going in the right direction or not; sensing an emotion that is about to bubble up in someone before they actually express it; and feeling drawn to an area of the body that has not been mentioned, but which you sense is in pain or needs your attention. You can then take action appropriate to your role with this person (a parent might be a comforting presence, whereas a healthcare provider might be taking therapeutic action.)

For those times when touch is used
in a professional treatment:

Touch in a Therapeutic Session

Let the body of the person you are with tell you what it needs.
You can do this by asking yourself: "What is the quality of
energy under my hands—does his or her energy meet me and
soak up what I have to offer easily, or does it initially push me
away?" "Where is energy flowing or not flowing?" "Are there
other images that come up when I lay my hands on this person's
body, such as fullness or emptiness, colors, textures, different
resonance?" Don't censor this incoming information; you can
always analyze it later if need be.

Witness Without An Agenda

Listen carefully to what is said during the time you are together.
Listen quietly; make soft, affirmative sounds to acknowledge
that you hear him or her. You might gently paraphrase back
what was said to be sure you heard correctly. Simply being
witnessed by another human being in this way is deeply healing,
in and of itself.

Honor Their Process and Pace

Honor the process and pace of the person you're working with.
Whether you are listening to someone share about growing up
with his mother's mental illness or helping a client deal with
the pain of multiple miscarriages, if you're holding a healing

space for someone's most ingrained, painful internal knot—one they've carried around for years—it may take more time to fully heal. Deep-seated physical and emotional tensions can take longer to resolve. It is not your job to judge the unfolding or pace of another person's healing, but rather, to be present for the healing that can happen in this moment. If you try to push too hard for resolution in an issue with many layers that have built up over years, you will most likely end up feeling exhausted and depleted, and the person you are trying to help will feel pushed or won't be able to fully integrate the work that you have done. Do what you can now and let the rest go.

Hold a Larger Vision

Maintain a vision of the person you are with as whole and healthy. At times, it may be appropriate to help the person remember how far they have come when they are feeling discouraged. This is as true for a child struggling in school with a learning disability as it is for an adult with chronic pain. It can be challenging to hold a vision of someone as healthy and whole when their problems are severe and multi-faceted. But it is essential that you do so. Learning to see that person's full potential and capacity to heal is one of the greatest gifts you can give.

Holding a space for possible healing does not mean having a Pollyanna attitude or giving false hope. It means recognizing that our innate capacity to heal is an unknown. I have seen remarkable healing take place that by all rights should not have been possible. So I never want to close the door to that possibility in someone's mind. I also recognize that 'healing' to a dying patient may look like that person's coming to terms with his life and dying peacefully, not healing his physical body.

Empower Them

Help the person you are with to get in touch with his or her own capacity for self-healing and empowerment. Your role is to be a compassionate witness, a loving guide. You may create the conditions in which healing can occur, but you are not the healer. The ultimate gift you can give is to help them uncover their own capacity to heal themselves. As they release tension and trauma from their tissues, they will naturally get more in touch with the things that nurture and nourish them in life and will begin to make healthier choices.

Considerations AFTER you have been present for another:

Recognize Their Changes

When you conclude, ask the person how they are feeling on a physical, mental, and emotional level. In the process of talking with them, you will be teaching them to pay attention to the subtle inner signals they need to discover and discern for themselves. For instance, as a parent, you might ask: "What is your confidence level now about giving that speech?" or "How are you feeling now, about the upcoming basketball game?" As a therapist you might ask: "What can you do differently in your life now, after the work we've just done together?"

As a healthcare practitioner, you might ask: "How is the

pain in your hip now, compared to when you came in?" or, "Your headache was a seven when you got here. Where is it now on a scale from 1 to 10? Has the quality or location of the pain changed?" By asking for specific information, you are helping them notice things they might have discounted before. You are empowering them to listen more effectively to their own internal landscape and take it out into their lives.

Acknowledge Their Commitment

Acknowledge their courage and commitment to heal. This can help them feel less passive and more like proactive partners in their own healing process. This is particularly important when someone is feeling discouraged by setbacks or slow progress.

Guide Them to See the Whole Picture

Help them stay aware of the bigger picture. Note the changes you see in them each time you are together compared to their earlier distress. Share any progress you have observed. People need feedback when they are not yet able to sense the shifts that you are picking up on. Often, when I point out some long-term changes to a client at the end of a session, they are pleasantly surprised, "Oh, yeah, that is true. I just wasn't paying attention to that." As a teacher or parent we are in a perfect position to hold and remind them of the larger screen of their lives and how they are progressing through it.

Help Them Plan Follow up Care

Make suggestions for supplemental or follow-up work—such as using the processes and exercises taught in this book—if appropriate. This might include your willingness to get together again or referrals to other practitioners or complementary approaches such as yoga, or working with a life coach or movement teacher. You might recommend journaling or a dream group. And psychotherapy, acupuncture, and other healthcare practitioners can be helpful in following through, supporting, or bringing to completion this person's healing process.

Hold an Attitude of Gratitude and Acceptance

Close with an attitude of gratitude and acceptance. This will help you stay in the present moment, rather than being caught up in regrets of things you didn't do or worries about what might happen with the person you were with. Acknowledge what you have done well, note the changes you would make if you see each other again in this context, and then let go of what is beyond your capacity to do at this time.

Remember Full Body Presence

Take care of yourself. Remember to end you time together with yourself feeling full. This might mean taking a few minutes to breathe deeply and feel the earth supporting and filling you up. It might mean closing with a silent prayer of appreciation for the healing and relaxation that has just transpired. It might also mean eating a snack or taking a short break or a walk or a relaxing bath. When you take care of you first, you are able to be fully present for others.

Therapeutic Presence in the Emergency Room

I recently heard from a friend, an emergency care physician who attended my Healing From the Core: Grounding and Healthy Boundaries training several years ago.

"Suzanne, had an interesting experience with a patient tonight in the ER—call me!"

Naturally I was intrigued, and minutes later we were talking. Here's what he told me.

> A nineteen year-old girl was brought in by her parents, unable to stop belching. It was constant—seconds between each burp. It had impaired her speech for days. She was quite upset, and things were getting worse, not better.

> After running all the proper tests to rule out more serious issues, my physician friend sat her down and asked her if she was willing to try something with him.

> At that point, she said she'd try anything. So the doctor took a moment to consciously remember his own grounding and full body presence. Then he proceeded to guide her to breathe through her nose rather than her mouth.

> Between his calm presence and her breathing, things in her body started to relax within minutes.

> He then slowly and calmly offered a series of suggestions that led her deeper into her body. Ultimately he got her awareness down to the ground under her, connecting her to the rich energy field of the earth and its relaxing and energizing qualities (he was using a shortened version of *Exploration II*).

All of fifteen minutes had passed as he held his calm, full body presence—and offered her access to her own.

"Suzanne, it was startling to see how easily and quickly her whole system relaxed and let go as I talked, right there in the ER!"

By the time he was finished, she was smiling. And she was no longer belching.

Then he let her know that she could do this for herself anytime she needed it. He referred her to resources that would enable her to replicate what they'd just done, and off she went—healthier and happier.

A calm, strong therapeutic presence is valuable in a variety of situations, even some that we might not ordinarily think of. But here's the big key: It needs to be enough of a habit for you so that it's easily accessible, even in the toughest situations.

It's the *being* state that helps any technique you *do* work more effectively, no matter where you are doing it!

Therapeutic Presence with Special Needs Children and their Parents

Kathleen is a pediatric speech pathologist with a successful practice in my area. She called to tell me this story about six months ago.

One of my most difficult, low-functioning, little patients, Gina, was brought in last week having the tantrum of all tantrums. Her mom was agitated and uncomfortable, and her little brother was cranky and irritable as well. I often see this with the families of special needs children who have loud tantrums as a way of expressing their frustrations. It is part of the child's coping mechanism with their inability to regulate themselves. The parents and siblings of these children often feel embarrassed and don't know what to do in response to this disruptive behavior.

Because I had just come back from one of your trainings, I decided to try something additional in Gina's session. Once I got Gina on my lap, I used your grounding and filling to create full body presence for myself so I could be a strong, steady presence in the room. First, I felt more relaxed, and then everyone else seemed to feel it as well. The deeper and wider I made my energy field presence, the more Gina calmed down. First she stopped crying. Then she made beautiful eye contact, and we had several moments of meaningful, purposeful interaction that she had never done before.

Then her brother, who normally demands his share of the attention when she gets agitated, became uncharacteristically calm and went off in a corner to play quietly with the toy trains. Usually, he would be dragging every toy across the room and expecting everyone else to engage with him about what he was doing. Later in the session, we were actually able to include him in our interactions. It is a huge therapeutic step for a child like Gina to have allowed this.

To top it all of, the mom completely relaxed and was smiling by the time they left. Later, she called to tell me that the three of them had a stress-free afternoon, which is unheard of for them.

The only variable that was different in Gina's session that day was that I added a conscious practice of grounding and filling throughout our therapy hour. I now incorporate my full body presence into every session I do. The parents of my patients have started to tell me that I consistently get a lot more done with their children than any of their other therapists. It is amazing how something as simple as grounding and filling can change the outcome of every session. This practice has made my life and my work more effective and easier all at the same time!

Practicing the Principles of Therapeutic Presence

Practicing the principles of therapeutic presence takes patience and ongoing commitment, but it is well worth the effort. It opens up a new model, or paradigm, of conscious awareness for helping others. Our lives are richest when we can be present to others in each moment, in a space of caring and compassion that enables us to receive as well as give. As an added bonus, the ability to serve as a presence for someone else's healing brings us into a deeper state of grace and resonance.

Everyone receives from this equation.
In this paradigm, to give is indeed to receive.

Chapter Ten

∾

Healing for Today
A World At Peace

In this closing chapter, using all the skills you have learned in this book, allow yourself to embody the vision that follows. Set your intention for the future from deeply in the present moment with a wide, full body presence. As you do this, you may find that your vision is different than mine. Record *your* vision. Drink it in. Receive it as fully as possible. And then live in accordance with it. Be an agent for change in the direction of your larger vision. Each of us has our specific gifts that are meant to be shared. Find yours and share it. Then walk in your world with heart-full courage, strength, and tenderness. And, enjoy!

Try reading the following aloud if possible.

Imagine a world where you get up in the morning with
energy to meet your day after a good night's rest.
Imagine you begin the day by checking in to make sure
your energy reservoir is as full as it can be.

Imagine your curiosity leading your day, so that your options stay open to whatever resources are available.

Imagine your heart having as much of a voice as your linear thought processes.

Imagine how it would be to feel steady and sure of yourself as you make decisions throughout your day.

Imagine being comfortable with *all* of yourself—feeling at home in your body and your world.

Imagine clarity of mind-body-spirit that guides your direction in the world—choosing from possibilities that not only feed you, but that are good for the rest of your world.

Imagine greeting the unfamiliar by being curious, awake, interested—but not fearful.

Imagine following your curiosity and creating in your world, using your natural gifts.

If you are not feeling well, imagine having the presence to check in with yourself and be a detective in your system so that you can get the best care possible.

Imagine knowing the questions to ask and getting the care you need.

Imagine taking the time to heal fully.

Imagine an ability to be friends with time—to slow down and enjoy your day, to rest and rejuvenate, *and* to effortlessly speed up and go for the goal when that is needed.

Imagine, as you meet the day, that you respond from inside your system. Your deeper creativity is acted upon.

Imagine you operate from a deep sense of love rather than a fear of change or others who are different from you.

Imagine being able to feel the tenderness in your heart and not being afraid of it.

Imagine feeling strong enough to feel what is in your heart and express it.

Imagine allowing your world to touch you deeply, drinking in the beauty that is around you—being able to soak up the love that is in your environment, rather than letting it pass by.

Imagine trusting your body and treating it like a valued friend and ally.

Imagine listening to, responding to, and following through with its care and healing.

Imagine allowing yourself to slow down and rest when you need it.

Imagine taking the time to enjoy your world—to celebrate and play.

Imagine feeling the strength and power of your lower body and being comfortable with it—in fact, deeply enjoying it.

Imagine having the wisdom to walk in your world with both your power and your tenderness.

Imagine being able to sense what kind of movement would be most healing and energizing that day.

Imagine feeling inspired to move in that way, rather than having to force yourself to exercise.

Imagine having your sexuality be a healthy, integrated part of you.

Imagine feeling comfortable with your sensuality— having enough nurturing touch in your life and happily receiving it.

Imagine a world where healing bodywork is readily available.

Imagine feeling deeply connected—a part of your environment.

Imagine valuing the natural world like a trusted family member.

Imagine a world where all decisions take the young, the old, and those without a voice into account. Where even the smallest of things are considered. Where resources *other* than money and size are the important deciding factors in any given moment.

Imagine a world where you are trusted and trustworthy.

Imagine a world that operates on trustworthiness— where it is held in high esteem. Where you learn to trust yourself and know how to trust others. You know from your inner gut feeling when something is really off or absolutely right on.

Imagine a world where, from a young age, you are helped to find your natural gifts and talents.

Imagine a world where you are then encouraged to explore and develop those gifts and talents as you grow.

Imagine a world where people become parents when they are ready, have the skills, and are supported in raising their children by their communities.

Imagine a world where people have access to the resources that nourish them—where they remember to slow down and take more time off periodically to feed their spirit, to sense into what is best for their higher good.
Imagine a world where people have the freedom and resources to join with others who are of like spirit and mind, to reconnect and rejuvenate at that level.
Imagine a world where people honor spiritual differences and learn from them.

Imagine a world where excellent healthcare is available when you need it, where your open communication with your own body is reflected in the larger system—your healthcare providers include your inner wisdom in their plan for care when you are out of balance or ill.

Imagine a world where international relations are built on the deeper understanding that we are all connected and that to survive and thrive, we must respond to each other knowing that what truly helps one side must help the other as well.

Imagine a world where we also have this understanding about our environment—where we treasure it, treat it with care and respect. Imagine a world where our food, air, earth, and water resources are pure, where they support healthy bodies and minds.

Imagine a world where our media systems—television, movies, the internet—educate us about what is healthy and help us to listen inside where we are encouraged to find our own unique gifts and style.

Imagine a world where the government is truly looking out for each person's wellbeing, the wellbeing of the environment, and the education and happiness of the people as a whole—where special interests are balanced and weighed against the good of the whole.

Imagine a system where your voice is heard and your vote matters.

Imagine the joy of living in full body presence.

Now that you have imagined all of this,
go out and live it. And enjoy!

Acknowledgements

∽

I t has taken a village to write this book. I am an oral
tradition person and making the shift from speaking to
writing has been a huge task for me. In doing this, an entire
village of friends, colleagues, family, students, and teachers have
helped me bring this book forward. It has been a project that
has spanned a decade and taken many forms along the way. I
want to remember and honor everyone who has contributed in
large and small ways along the path, so here goes.

My first thanks must go to Kari Uman for helping me write
my initial version of the Five Principles and Peggy Linden for
helping me write my first study guide—both invaluable
beginning steps. Then there were a series of excellent writers
who mid-wifed my writing process at different points along the
way—thank you to Kim Falone, Kay Schaefer, Jodi Carlson,
Carol Goldsmith, Lulu Torbet, Maureen O'Neill, Laura Davis
and my final, book-birthing, writer, Ja-lene Clark. And thanks
to my original illustrator, Kay Hansen, and my designer and
illustrator for this book, David Andor. Right behind these are
my instructors and presenters, many of whom donated hours to
days pouring over the materials to help me clarify and organize.
So, a *huge* thanks goes out to Joanna Haymore, Kathy Burns,
Angela Stevens, Lori Chinitz, Amelia Mitchell, Cari Rowan,
Gene Miller, Dale Kressley, Richard Griffin, Sandy Brown, Deb
Schneider-Murphy, and Tamara Blossic.

The rest of the village—some who donated a lot of time
brainstorming or editing my writing at key points in this
process—get my next wave of gratitude. A huge thank-you goes

to the loving efforts of my women's group (you know who you are), Jane Luce, Karen Hale, Kay Shubert, Karen Copeland, John Hoernemann, Chris Slate, Susie Steiner, Tim Hutton, Maryalice Fischer, Cheri Bailey, Connie Wells, Christi Fath, Diana Walker, Julie Johns, Deb Wahl, Laura Mitchell, Cosper Scafidi, Carol Duffner, and Donna Setzer.

I am sure there are others I am forgetting. It has been a decade of asking for and receiving help from my entire village. Thank you all from the bottom of my heart.

I could not have completed this book without my dedicated Healing From the Core office support team's efforts in keeping it all running across the last decade: Lynn (and Tim) Foley, Jan Yates, B.J. Frame, Robin Heimburg, Cynthia Schell, Deb Krahling, Monique Roberts, Carol Molesky, and Elizabeth Charles. Some of you actually had a desk in the office and others supported me from behind the scenes, but you all were wonderful—thanks!

Then the next great wave of gratitude goes out to all the students and clients whose experiences have enriched my life and this book. Your stories have taught me valuable lessons that were passed forward here.

And, finally, the biggest wave of gratitude goes to my family members who have supported and encouraged me throughout this entire process—my husband, Carlos; my daughter, Alieza; my son, Aren; my mother, Mary Jane; and my sister, Debbie. Your patience and love (and shoulder massages) have been invaluable resources for me. You keep me going. I love you all.

Appendix:

Transcriptions of Audio Explorations

~

Introduction

The following audio program accompanies the book, *Full Body Presence: Explorations, Connections and More to Experience Present Moment Awareness* by Suzanne Scurlock-Durana. In this program, Suzanne presents three *Explorations*—the directions for how to use them optimally are in the book.

As a reminder, do not listen to any of these Explorations *while driving a car or operating other heavy machinery, as these* Explorations *lead listeners into a deep state of relaxation and can cause drowsiness.*

TRANSCRIPT OF EXPLORATION I

Opening Awareness:
Where Am I In This Moment?

∽

Welcome to *Exploration I, Opening Awareness*—"Where Am I in *This* Moment?"

My name is Suzanne Scurlock-Durana, and I'll be your guide throughout this series.

Begin by settling in, gliding into neutral, releasing your expectations, agendas, and judgments. Allow yourself to naturally, effortlessly respond to the following suggestions and questions, knowing that the ideal response is whatever spontaneously shows up in your body, your conscious awareness, as we go. The nature of your experience will naturally change and deepen as this process unfolds and with repeated practice.

Choose a comfortable seat with good back support and let your feet rest easily and fully on the floor. Take a moment now to get comfortable and then we'll begin.

As you close your eyes or partially close your eyes, turning your attention inward, gather your awareness, your openness to discovery, and let it travel in with your breath, following your inhalation down into your lungs... settling your conscious awareness *inside* your body—and letting the external world fall away....

Let's begin by taking a baseline reading—an *overall* look—inwardly scanning your entire body from head to toe, being curious about anything that pops into your awareness, noting areas that feel at ease—comfortable; in other words, where you *feel more connection*. You may notice sensations of warmth or coolness, a sense of fullness or spaciousness—allow yourself to take in these sensations, no matter how subtle. Take a few moments now to notice any area or areas where you *feel more connection*. (Pause for 15 seconds.)

Then notice the internal areas that feel *less present*—where there is less sensation, pain, or numbness. Just noticing, without judgment. You may notice discomfort or a lack of feeling. Certain areas just may simply feel more distant. Noticing anywhere that you feel *less* connected right now. Internally scanning, relaxed... (Pause 15 seconds.)

You are taking a baseline *sensory* snapshot of how you *feel overall* as you begin. (Pause for 15 seconds.)

Now bring your attention back to your breath and allow yourself to be *curious* about the subtle sensations of breathing. Notice the *temperature* of the air as it enters your nose and throat, traveling down into your lung... is it cool or warm? Feeling the rise and fall of your ribs... Is there anywhere that your breathing feels restricted, or is it easy and full?

As you inhale and exhale, do you notice your chest rising and falling, or are you more aware of your back resting against the chair? In other words, is more of you present right now in the front of you or in the back? Or do you feel them both equally?

Allow your attention to move up into your neck and head. What do they feel like?

What do your eyes feel like? Is there any sense of strain or are they relaxed? How does the air around you feel on your cheeks?

What does your mouth feel like? Is your jaw tight or

relaxed? How do your teeth and gums and tongue feel? Hmmmmm.

How does your neck feel right now? Does one side feel more relaxed than the other? How does your throat feel?

Returning to your chest, notice your breathing again for a moment... with your deepening awareness, do you notice any changes? How does the rise and fall of your ribs feel *now*? Hmmm.

How does your *heart* feel? Allow yourself to feel the sensations in your heart area with as little interpretation as possible—can you feel it beating? Be aware of all the different ways *you* receive sensation. Does your heart *feel* like a particular color?

And letting your attention spread out from the heart area, allow yourself to notice the sensations in the rest of your chest ... and on out to your shoulders... your upper back... down your arms into your hands and fingers. . . . How do your arms and hands feel? Heavy or light? Distant or connected to your chest and heart? Pulsating or vibrating? How do your arms and hands feel right now?

When you are ready, allow your attention to return to your breath... letting your awareness drop *down* as you exhale... settling into your torso... deeper and wider with each exhale... noticing... Does one side of your torso feel denser or lighter than the other? Bigger or smaller? Or are things balanced equally? Is there a particular texture or color or pulsation that you sense anywhere in your torso?... Hmmm, ...

Do you have a *sense* of your backbone leaning against the chair? Do you feel more up in your neck area... or lower down, in your sacrum, or does your energy feel the same throughout? Allow yourself to move gently, if you wish, in order to feel more in your spine. Does your spine feel solid and steady...or is there less sensation here? Notice how connected you feel to the bones of your spine right now. No judgment. Simply noticing... good....

Now allow your attention to drop down to your pelvis—to your connection to the chair you're sitting on. What is the sensation of your sitting bones contacting the chair? Is one side resting more fully than the other, or are they balanced equally?

Notice the sensation in your upper legs, of your thighs, resting on the chair. Do they feel connected to your body? Can you sense the *bones* of your thighs?

And your knees? Do they feel different from each other or the same? Stiff or flexible? Do you sense any particular colors or textures?

How about your calves? What do they feel like? Do you have a sense of them being a long way from your head and torso, or do they feel connected and strong? Do they feel alike, or is one more relaxed than the other? Or denser than the other?

How do your feet feel? Notice if the sensations are different or the same for both feet. What do your toes feel like? Do you feel your heels as keenly as you feel the arches and balls of your feet? Are both feet resting easily and fully on the floor, or does one feel more connected than the other?... Simply noticing... Good....

Now take a moment to scan through your entire system again, taking another overall broad-brush look at your internal landscape, as you did when you began. As your awareness deepens, what are you noticing? Are there any changes since you first scanned your body? Take note of any sensory information: colors—textures—areas of dark or lightness—symmetries or asymmetries... being curious and simply noticing.

When you are done, let your awareness return to the outer world... gently open your eyes and notice how the world around you feels now, compared to when you began... and thank yourself for taking this time to deepen your *internal* awareness.

TRANSCRIPT OF EXPLORATION II:

Grounding and Filling: Nourishing and Replenishing the Container of Your Being

Let yourself begin by settling in. And as this process unfolds, allow yourself to naturally, effortlessly respond to the following suggestions and questions, knowing that the ideal response is whatever spontaneously shows up in your body and in your conscious awareness as we go. *Exploration II* is the core practice of the embodiment process. The nature of your experience will naturally change and deepen with repeated practice.

Again, make yourself comfortable, with your eyes closed or partially closed and your feet resting easily and fully on the floor. And again, invite your curiosity—your openness to discovery—to lead your conscious awareness in this *Exploration*, so you can release any expectations or judgments as you go.

Following your breath, allow your awareness to drop into your internal landscape, feeling the rise and fall of your ribcage with each inhale... and exhale... breathing normally and noticing the sensations... the temperature of the air in your nostrils, the feel of the air traveling down into your lungs... your chest rising and falling... the feeling of your backbone on the chair... simply noticing, being curious....

Where *are you more present* in your body in this moment and where are you *not*—where there is ease and comfort or... numbness or pain? Take a sensory snapshot that gives you a beginning reference point.

Breathing comfortably, allow your awareness to drop on

down through your torso.... Are your sitting bones resting equally on the chair?

How do your knees feel today? Hmmmm....

How do your feet feel resting on the floor? Simply notice— no judgment.

(pause)

Now we are going to make contact with the earth, right down through the floor and into the ground, connecting with its rich and abundant energy. Allow your awareness to drop down beneath your feet, into the earth's field as though you were putting down roots of awareness, or perhaps light beams of awareness, or maybe riding a river of awareness—use whichever imagery works for you. What does the earth feel like under you? Let sensations come without judgment.... Is it cool or warm? Is it hard-packed and rocky? Or are you moving through sand or loose soil? Give yourself permission to take in these sensations, even if you don't know exactly where they're coming from....

Now, allow your awareness to go *deeper* into the earth, as though there is no resistance. Traveling down your *roots* or *light beams* or flowing on your *river* of awareness—going as deeply as it feels *comfortable* for *you* right now... (pause)... Perhaps your roots are on their way to the core of the earth, or you may be spreading a carpet of tiny roots right on the earth's surface. Or in this moment you may just be able to feel the earth touching your feet, but may not yet be comfortable extending your awareness down into it... *Wherever you are is fine.* Simply notice what sensations show up when you get curious as to what the earth feels like under you... (pause)... Allow yourself to notice that you can feel this connection outside of yourself that's safe, unconditional, and supportive.

And, if you are feeling any excess tension, give yourself permission to simply let it go. You can take a deep breath and exhale the tension... (inhale and exhale deeply). Or you can allow it to flow like water, down and out into the earth.... Or, you can release it through the pores of your skin, like moisture evaporating on a cool breeze... simply allowing yourself to *let go* of whatever *excess tension you may have, whatever you no longer need*.

Hmmmm... And now, setting the intention to receive *only* what is most nurturing and nourishing, starting at your feet, invite the earth's energy field to begin to fill your body—your container—by asking yourself, "What would feel most nurturing and nourishing in my feet right now?

Warmth or coolness? Do you feel a deep pulsation or maybe a high-pitched humming? Be alert to *all* sensory cues... hmmm....

Does it feel like a particular color? Perhaps a cool blue-green or a warm red-orange or some other color?

Allow your feet to gently fill, letting nurturing sensation come up through the earth and in through your skin, soaking into all your muscles, ligaments and tendons, letting every cell fill, all the way in to the very core of your bone marrow and all the way out to your skin. Bones are like sturdy sponges, filled with many tiny air spaces. So allow your bones to soak up this nurturing, nourishing energy as though they were sponges soaking up clean, clear water.

Your feet *may* feel like they are becoming longer and wider as they fill. You may notice that one foot fills more fully or a little more quickly than the other. Or, you may simply experience an increased awareness—as you *intend* to let your feet receive nurturing sensation, they may simply feel different...

Do your best not to judge how much or how little you may be feeling.

Let your curiosity come forward and then notice what sensations show up....

Moving at a pace that works for you, invite that nourishing feeling up into your ankles.... Again, allow the sensation to soak all the way into your bones and all the way out to your skin... hmmmm...

How about your shins and calves? What would feel most nurturing there? Coolness or warmth, pulsating or humming? Perhaps the sensation—the feeling—of a long, slow stretch? Allow yourself to receive whatever sensation would nourish your calves and shins right now... letting all your cells fill up and plump out—feeling juicy.

What would feel most healing and energizing in your knees?... Let *that* sensation permeate all the nooks and crannies of your knees... soaking up this replenishing energy.

And, as we go along, if there is an area that has a harder time receiving nurturing sensation, simply notice it, allow that place to receive what it can, and cradle it gently with your awareness. Then move on, always going at your own pace.

How about your thighs? Allow this nourishing sensation to soak from the bone marrow of your thighs all the way out to your skin... letting it flow from the earth up through your feet and calves and knees right into your thighs... good....

Allow a sense of safe, nurturing sensation to begin to fill your pelvis.... What would feel most nourishing and healing to your sitting bones, your hip bones, your sacrum—that V-shaped bone at the base of your spine... the entire pelvic bowl ... soaking up this nourishment like a sponge in a clear pool of water... (sound of soaking up)....

And what would feel most nurturing and energizing in your belly? Take a nice deep breath, cradle this area with your awareness, and let it fill and relax. Allow yourself to experience this area, because there's plenty of wonderful energy to be awakened here.

Yes....You may feel the area around and under your navel, gently opening, filling up from your legs, into your belly, and then moving all the way back to your spine, and all the way out to your sides. Letting all your reproductive organs and the other organs of your belly and midsection soak up what they need to feel energized and relaxed and full of life... hmmmm....

And if you notice your mind wandering for a moment, simply bring your attention back—*Oh, yes, I was nurturing my belly*... taking the time to slow down and nurture myself.

Let this flow of nourishing energy permeate your spine.... Is it warm or cool? Does it feel like a particular color? Notice as each vertebra, all the way up, and the spinal cord inside the vertebral canal, soak up whatever would feel most healing and relaxing right now... hmmmm....

It's helpful to breathe easily and as deeply as you can during this phase, because the breath moves the spine from the inside out and gives you more sensory awareness of it. (Inhale and exhale.) Also, feeling your spine against the chair or whatever is supporting you gives you even more sensory information about your backbone....

If you find any area where there is pain, you may notice that for a moment or two the pain intensifies. If so, just simply allow yourself to *be with it* as best you can. You're not trying to change or force the pain out; you're just gently sitting with it and allowing it to receive whatever nurturing and nourishing energy it can in this moment. And you may find that where the rest of your body wants a rosy red color, an area that's in pain may seem to want some other color, perhaps a nice cool blue, green, or a clear silver color.... Allow it to soak up whatever nurturing it can...

Now, what would feel most nurturing in your chest... your lungs... and your heart? Perhaps the sense of an easy full breath (inhale and exhale), bringing fresh oxygen to your lungs and then your heart and on out to all your cells as you inhale and exhale... (inhale and exhale audibly)... hmmmm... nice....

And what would feel most relaxing and energizing to your shoulders... your upper chest and back? I often summon the the feeling of snuggling in a soft blanket. What would feel most nourishing to *you* right here in *your* shoulders right now?

(pause)

Continue to relax and receive the sensations of nourishing yourself... taking in only what is most nurturing to you *right now*.... Often your mind doesn't know the answer when you ask internally— and yet a sensation shows up that feels relaxing or energizing or nurturing... Simply open and receive it as best you can... hmmmm....

And what would feel most relaxing and energizing in your arms... your upper arms... your elbows... your forearms... down into your hands? You can gently let your fingers stretch out to draw the nurturing flow down your arms into your hands and fingers... hmmmm....

And what would feel most nourishing to your neck and throat? Coolness or warmth? Perhaps a sensation of spaciousness or movement? What would feel most healing and energizing here? Allow yourself to receive it as fully as you can right now ... hmmmmm....

What about your face... your jaw... your eyes? What

sensation would feel most relaxing and nurturing here? Hmmm....

Allow that nurturing sensation to filter all the way through to the back of your head, filling and relaxing your entire brain, all the membranes and surrounding structures and bones... filling and being energized.

Tune in to this flow of nurturing energy filling you... filling all of you... coming in from the earth under you, through your feet and legs, through your torso and neck, arms and hands, all the way up into your head, filling and nurturing you all the way up to the crown of your head... until it begins to move out the crown, showering down around you like a gentle fountain, bathing your skin and the energy field that runs through it and around it....

If your head feels a little closed at the top, like a slight sensation of pressure, gently and slowly pull up on your right there at the crown until you feel it open... allowing that river of energy to flow out, showering down around you.

So we're nearing the end of this *Exploration*.

(pause)

When you're ready, gently notice how you feel *now* compared to when you began. Simply notice.

You've just connected, grounding into the earth, receiving its nourishment and support. You have created a fuller, stronger energy field within yourself, and bathed in it for quite a while. You have strengthened your personal boundaries, the membrane between you and the world. This allows you to connect more deeply when you choose to and feel strong enough to say "no" when you need to. It gives you clarity to see yourself and the world around you and the energy to cope with whatever arises. Notice how you feel *now* compared to when you began. This nourishing energy is always available to you through this process and is your core access to building a strong, nurturing container for your own life's energy and pleasure....

And when you're ready, bring your awareness back from the internal to the external. Feel your feet on the floor as you open your eyes. Allow yourself to *drink* in your surroundings, being informed and nurtured by all you see.

Yes.... Good.... Enjoy!

TRANSCRIPT OF EXPLORATION III
Healing the Internal Resistance to Life

∽

Welcome to *Exploration III*. This *Exploration* is done in three segments. You may stop after any of the three segments or go all the way through. The first segment explores a physical place of resistance. The second segment addresses limiting beliefs and painful recurring thoughts. And the third segment is on healing relationships. They are in this order because they build on each other. You will be given the option to stop the session at the end of each segment (signaled by a 10-second silence), or you can cruise on through the entire *Exploration*.

So make yourself comfortable, with good back support and your feet planted easily and fully on the floor, readjusting your position as needed during the process, eyes closed or slightly open. Allow your mind to glide into neutral, releasing any expectations, agendas, or judgments you may be aware of right now. As best you can, let yourself simply experience this process.

Take a couple of easy breaths, settling back into your body. Scan through your whole internal landscape, noticing all the sensations and textures—easily filling and energizing, connecting to the earth or whatever unconditional resource works best for you at this time, so that you are beginning this *Exploration* full and energized.

(pause)

(slowly) Now, bring to your awareness the area of your body where you feel most at home, where you feel a strong sense of

connection. It might be your heart ... or your belly.... . It might be your feet ... or your pelvis ... or your hands. It could be your backbone.... . Wherever you feel the strongest sense of presence, let your awareness go and rest in that place right now and feel the fullness, the strength of that place. It will probably feel very comfortable to be there. It is easy to rest into this place.

Take a moment now to soak up a little more from the earth's field of energy—allowing nourishing sensation into this area, so that it begins to expand and spread out.

And in this place of strength and presence, let yourself feel or see or sense a ball of healing presence or energetic healing hands—emitting energy that is loving, patient, nurturing, strong, yet soft. This place contains unconditional love for you, which you may feel as comfort or support in some way. So if energy hands feel right for you, use that. If a ball of healing presence works best for you, work with that image.

Sense or feel or see this healing energy in whatever way you can. Sometimes you just know that it's there. Even if you don't know how you know, that's fine.... . Some of you will be able to vividly see this healing presence or your energy hands; you'll have a color, a pulsation, a texture. Some of you will clearly feel this healing presence. You'll feel the warmth and strength. Simply allow yourself to have an awareness of this energy presence, in whatever way you can. Yes ... good.

Next, ask to be shown what block or place of resistance in your body would be best for you to work with today. Notice what pops into your conscious awareness after you've asked. It may be a surprise to you, or it may be a familiar place, a place where you've often felt resistance or pain. You may feel a restricted sensation in this place or a sense of disconnection from the energy flow in the surrounding areas. You may know exactly where this is—or you may need to look around a little, asking your body to show you more clearly. Sometimes there will be pain or numbness there, or maybe it's a place that resonates with a limiting or painful phrase you often hear in your head. Perhaps you experience it as a place of trapped emotion such as grief or·rage, sadness or shame. If you discover more than one troubled area, ask to be shown which one would be best for you to work with today. Trust what your body shows you.

Feel the edges of this place. Does it have a color? Does it have a shape? Notice ... notice ... What size is it? If it begins to feel overwhelming, let it rest back in your consciousness for a moment, and take your awareness back to your place of greatest strength and comfort, and then down to your feet, tuning up your connection to the unconditional rich energy field of the earth. Good... .

When you are ready, allow your awareness to return to that part of you where you feel most at home—and to the ball of healing presence or the energy hands that live in that area of your body where you feel most connected. Allow this healing presence, your energy hands, to expand from your place of strength and to gently cradle the place that feels painful or disconnected or resistant—gently, with no expectations. If your actual physical hands can hold this place easily and without straining, allow them to join your energy hands or presence in cradling this spot.

These hands are not here to change this resistant part of you—your healing presence has no agenda. It is simply loving, caring, and strong—unconditionally holding and loving the part of you that feels disconnected (perhaps feeling hurt, ashamed, or unworthy in some way.)

If you are holding a physical sensation of pain, like a lump of grief in your throat, or an area of pain in your heart, or a clutch of fear in your gut, just gently cradle that place and let the pain or the grief or the fear or the shame emerge at its own pace to connect with the healing energy hands or presence. There is no goal to change anything. Your pain and resistance is there for some reason. And perhaps that reason is outdated— there was a valid reason when it began, and it may now be a defense you no longer need. It's not important to understand it now. Simply hold it and love it. Loving in the agape definition of love—all encompassing, unconditional love for yourself ... as though you were cradling a sleeping kitten, or puppy... .

Just gently hold it... . You are simply there to be with that aspect of yourself. You are not doing anything to it. You're not going to throw it away. You're not going to try to make it disappear. You are simply there with it.

This can be challenging, particularly if you are holding a place of chronic pain. You may already feel more aware and connected to that painful place than you want to be, habitually feeling the edges of it and managing your day around it. But if you can allow yourself to go deeper today, you'll find that you are not truly connected with this place. You have been holding it at bay, controlling it—in order to be able to tolerate it. So let the edges of the pain just gently be with those energy hands or that healing presence. Simply be present, connecting with the pain, with the grief, with the sadness, whatever it is.

And if you start to feel overwhelmed by the emotion or the pain, let it take a back seat for a moment and return to feeling your feet on the ground, feeling the energy flowing up through your body, backing up the support of your healing energy hands or presence, restoring the strong, safe container around the process, around this issue that's going on. And when you're ready, return to gently cradling it ... noticing what happens. Noticing what happens as you hold it. No expectations. Often, this is the hardest part. Your mind may have a different agenda that sounds like this.

"Oh, but I want to get rid of it."

"Oh, but I'm so tired of this pain."

"Oh, I hate this feeling."

Whatever the words are, let them go on by. Let the judgment go and allow yourself to simply be there, connecting more and more with that part as best you can in this moment.

Accepting "what is" without letting it drive your bus or take over your existence. Reminding yourself that this place of pain or grief is not all of you; it is only a part of you. You also have your feet under you, you have your energy flowing and surrounding this area, you have this strong energy presence holding and loving this part of you as best you can at this point. As best you can. Hmm... .

And as things begin to soften and change, remind yourself to simply be with this place—don't slip into doing something with it. Remember the un-conditionality that you're offering this part of you. Consciously we do not want this pain or emotion, but these are deep, long held patterns that require our patience and compassion to transform.

In my experience, one of the most effective ways to have pain change in a permanent way is to learn how to find a way to release it from its tightened down state—unlocking it from its prison. To do this you need to become one with it—to connect with it deeply, so that it can be free to heal.

So check in again....

How is it feeling now?

What's happening?

Hmm.... . Yes... . Yes... . Notice as things change, as they evolve ... honoring your own pace ... holding that place in your awareness, cradling and loving it unconditionally ... allowing whatever arises to unfold. Don't stand in the way. If you notice the edges of your painful place starting to spread out and disperse, let it happen—widen your cradling presence, creating a larger space for it, so that it can evolve and transform when it is ready. Staying connected to it, but allowing it to heal and change at its own pace ... so integration is more complete when it finally occurs ... hmmmm ... yeah... .

And notice how this place feels now compared to when you began this process ... allow yourself to notice the small subtle changes as well as the big ones. Just simply being with this place with gratitude for all the healing, large and small, that may have occurred here today.

And, gently let this place know that you will continue to hold it with loving presence, even though your conscious awareness may be elsewhere. And let this part of you know that you have made a commitment to reconnect with it and that your internal healing presence, your energy hands, will stay with this place as long as is required to heal and transform and reconnect with the rest of you ... until it is completely integrated ... whether that process takes a few minutes or a few months or a few years ... you are now committed to healing and integrating this part of you back into the whole.

Additional Script I:

Working With Limiting Beliefs

∼

Now let's work with the way in which your mind and, specifically, your limiting beliefs and painful thoughts come into this process. Most of us are aware of the inner critical voice that can plague us with doubting, shaming, chiding, even insulting thoughts, often denigrating our self-worth or questioning our right to exist.

To begin, bring to mind one of your painful thoughts or limiting beliefs—perhaps the one associated with the physical place of resistance that you just held and loved... or, notice any limiting or painful thought that is bothering you right now.

Notice where you feel that thought reverberating in your body. Where does it anchor in your system? Oftentimes a very painful thought will reverberate or be anchored in a pretty specific area like your heart, or in a part of your body where you may have chronic pain, or a place that was traumatized at some point in the past, like your throat or belly, or anywhere actually. Simply notice where the connection is between the painful or limiting thought and your body. If it seems to connect to everywhere, notice where the connection seems the strongest or densest... it may be a familiar place....

Wherever the anchor of your pain or discomfort is, allow your internal healing presence, your energy hands, to come and cradle that place as we proceed, loving it as unconditionally as you can in this moment. No agenda—simply being present with it—holding it gently and witnessing it in the kind, unconditional way you just finished practicing.

Now, silently repeating your limiting belief or painful thought... ask yourself....

"Am I sure that this limiting belief is true?"

Can you open to the possibility that this thought is not true at some level?

Really you don't know whether it's true or not, even though you may have a lot of data from past history to back up the fact that it might have been true at some point, you really don't know whether it is still true.

So now ask yourself,

"What would it feel like if I were open to the possibility that this painful thought or limiting belief is not true? What would it feel like?"

And make this question very specific to whatever your painful thought is. For example, if the thought is "I am not good enough," you might say instead,

"I'm open to the possibility that this thought of not being good enough is just not true. I'm open to the possibility that I am good enough."

When you are ready, you can go a step farther and say,

"I'm open to the possibility that not only am I good enough, but that who I am is a pleasure ... is a pleasure."

Notice how that feels inside when you can say that to yourself and sit with it, believing it, if only for a moment.

Letting all internal judgments go silent.

What does it feel like in your body?

What's the sensation in the area now being cradled by those wonderful energy hands? Notice... Notice....

What would it feel like in your body if you could suspend

that limiting belief and feel the ways in which you are a pleasure?

Allow that area to fully receive that possibility, even if it is only for a short while right now. Allow yourself to open even more to that possibility....

(pause)

What does that feel like? Feeling that you truly are a pleasure....

(pause)

Can you feel any of the tightness dissipating?

(pause)

Can you feel the more ease in this place?

(pause)

Can you feel any expansion inside as your perceptual lens expands?

(pause)

Allow the healing process to unfold... Good....

(pause)

This process takes positive affirmations all the way to the core of your being, because you are actually feeling in your body—physically sensing—what it is like to open to new possibilities. This allows you to heal not just mentally, but emotionally and physically and, thus, spiritually as well.... Good....

And notice how this place feels now compared to when you began this process... allow yourself to notice the small subtle changes as well as the big ones. Just simply being with this place with gratitude for all the healing, large and small, that may have occurred here today.

And let this place you've been holding and loving—and dialoguing with—gently know that you will continue to hold it with loving presence, even though you may not have it in your conscious awareness as you go on back out into your life.

And, you may want to commit to returning to this *Exploration* tomorrow and perhaps the next day if something still remains that needs your conscious attention to bring it to completion. So take a moment and see what commitment, no matter how small, you want to make to yourself in terms of this healing process, and then commit to it for as long as it takes.

Additional Script II:

Working with Interpersonal Issues— Relationships

This process also works with issues that are on an interpersonal level. Not surprisingly, stresses and problems in relationships are often the source of great internal pain and discomfort. Right now, you might be carrying around a ball of fear or anger or shame or grief from a fight with your spouse or your teenager, with a work colleague or your best friend. When this occurs, you know that in this relationship something is just not working. The energy is not flowing between you—the connection is not there the way you want it to be.

The following segment will help you shift how you relate to this situation or relationship pattern, starting with your own reactions and moving on to finding new healing possibilities for yourself and perhaps for the other people involved.

Take a moment now to tune up your connection to the earth and make sure you are feeling full and energized.

Next, bring to mind the person, situation or relationship pattern that feels painful or uncomfortable to you right now. As that sinks in, allow yourself to notice the underlying painful thought, the limiting phrase—the internal words— that go along with this person or situation. It might be similar to the limiting belief you just worked with or it could be something like:

"I'm just unlovable."

Or, "I am not safe."

Or, "I feel overwhelmed."

Or, "I'm being abandoned."

When a belief like this dominates your thinking, it narrows your perceptual lens, keeping you from feeling the good connections you want to have with this person. Take a moment now and look for the words that reverberate through you to that ball of painful emotion in your body somewhere.

(pause)

And once again, bring your internal nurturing hands or healing energy presence to that tight place in your body where your limiting belief is anchored and hold it unconditionally and lovingly as you've done in the previous *Exploration*s... good....

Then begin to expand your perceptual lens on this issue by saying something like:

"I'm open to the possibility that this relationship could be different, that this relationship could heal—could have pleasure in it again. I'm open to the possibility that I could be connected in a healthy way with my husband/teenager/ friend/colleague."

Now, the tricky part of this is to hold that possibility, and expand your perceptual lens without letting your left brain jump in immediately trying to problem-solve and figure it all out. Your challenge is to stay in an open feeling state, keeping your expansion and awareness in the realm of possibility, keeping it in the soft, diffuse place where the creativity to resolve the problem will begin to stir and show you the next step in a healing direction, or perhaps even the whole picture.

So you just hold the thought, "I'm open to the possibility. I have no idea what it would look like. Even if in my conscious mind, I cannot imagine how this could be true, I'm open to the possibility that this relationship could heal and be a pleasure again, that it could work, that we could have a connection again around this issue or in this particular area. I don't know how, but I'm open to that possibility."

And then pay attention to what happens in your body. Feel your feet. Feel your torso. Feel your shoulders. Feel the place being cradled by your loving, powerful energy hands. Allow it to shift and change as you feel into this new possibility. Simply cradling it, loving it, and letting go of judgments as they show up.

When you are able to open your perceptual field and you are willing, really willing, to be open to new possibilities, things are bound to unfold in some very interesting ways in your being.

From my own experience, both personally and as a teacher, many longstanding or complex issues, between couples especially, are not so quickly and easily resolved, Sometimes I will need to hold the possibility for healing and reconnection for weeks or months, through many repetitions of this *Exploration*, before I can really begin to feel in a clear solid way the direction that I need to go in to create that healing, because my resistance and my ego are so strongly attached to the problem. Perhaps I don't want to admit that I've made a mistake or was wrong about something. Or I don't want to admit to myself, or to my partner, my part in the process that has separated us. So, although the steps in this process are pretty straightforward, it's not necessarily an easy path to take.

Consistent effort—persistence in using the process, trusting that there is an answer somewhere, and holding open the possibility are the keys here. When you add these to the kindness and gentleness of the unconditional presence you are holding for yourself, you have a winning combination.

Or, if you feel particularly stuck or hopeless, the following phrase can be helpful:

"I'm open to the possibility that this issue is not as it seems, that I am missing something, that there may be another way to see this—the whole truth of this issue may not yet be evident."

Sit quietly with these words and be open to new information. See what pops into your awareness. Watch your dreams. Ask to be shown the whole picture, open again, and listen for the still small voice of deeper wisdom to whisper to you.

Another effective tactic in resolving these stubborn, painful situations is to make a commitment to remember the possibility that you're holding, as you go through each day, in your contact with this person or with the issues that bring up the pain or discomfort within yourself.

Make a commitment to remember it differently.

Make a commitment to be open to the possibility, to expand your perceptual lens around this particular issue, so that if there is another truth to be seen, it will show itself.

And sometimes when we are feeling stuck, we have to look in the mirror. Is a part of you fighting this process because you don't want to admit your role in it? Can you gently hold that part of you and look it in the eyes and admit to yourself that you do have a role in this situation... and without blame or criticism, simply acknowledge it and move on to creating a solution—a new way of seeing yourself and the other person in this situation.

Sometimes as your perceptual lens expands, you are suddenly able to hear people around you telling you things that can help you see your issue in a new way—things that you weren't open to hearing before. And then events spontaneously happen around you that show you things—that help you to see things with new eyes.

When we're present, with our eyes wide open, we learn from everything that happens in our lives, rather than just repeating the same events over and over again. None of us want our most painful events to be repeated over and over. We often just don't see any other way. So make a commitment to be open to the possibility that you could see things in a new way.

Take a moment now and check in again with part of you being cradled by your internal healing hands or presence. How does it feel now? As you've considered new possibilities and expanded your perceptual lens, how has that impacted this place? Has it started to shift and expand a little, or a lot? Are you feeling the edges of some new ways to see your situation? Good.... Wherever you are with this is fine.

And sometimes the most important step in resolving a tangled, seemingly intractable relationship problem is to make a commitment to set aside time to do this *Exploration* on a regular basis so that you have a vehicle to move your issue toward resolution, step by step, while holding yourself in a loving, powerful way. So take a moment to commit to whatever you need to do, no matter how small, if this issue needs more conscious air time from you.

And let this part of you know that, although you are going to take your conscious awareness elsewhere as we finish up, you remain committed to this healing process as long as it takes... whether it takes a few minutes or a few months or a few years.

And now, bring your awareness back to your feet and feel the earth beneath you, soaking up what you need in order to end this process full, with that flow moving through you, feeling ready to bring your awareness back from the internal to the external, feeling full and juicy.

(pause)

When you are ready, open your eyes and drink in your surroundings. Feel your backbone against your chair. Feel the steadiness of your body. Notice how you feel now compared to when you began.

·And... enjoy!

Resources

~

We now actually live in a world where the imaginings written in Chapter Ten are possible. The available resources and conscious awareness about all of these issues is now growing so quickly that I have added a resource page to my website. This allows these lists to be continually updated. Please visit:

www.FullBodyPresence.com

I encourage you to also sign-up for the newsletter to learn about new and exciting resources as they become available.

It is up to us to choose to go for it, and enjoy!

To order additional copies of this book, visit the website above or contact:

Healing From the Core Media
PO Box 2534,
Reston, VA 20195-2534

About the Author

~

SUZANNE SCURLOCK-DURANA, C.M.T, C.S.T.-D has taught about conscious awareness and its relationship to the healing process for over 25 years. She is passionate about teaching people practical skills that allow them to feel the joy of being present in each moment of their lives, without burning out.

She is a certified instructor of CranioSacral Therapy and SomatoEmotional Release with the Upledger Institute. Based on decades of teaching healthcare practitioners how to hold a healing space for themselves and others, Suzanne developed the Healing From the Core curriculum and complementary audio series. She teaches both curriculums internationally. She also provides ongoing staff development training at the Esalen Institute and collaborates regularly with Emilie Conrad, integrating Continuum movement with healing presence.

Known for her honest, grounded, nurturing manner, Suzanne assists others in going to the heart of their healing process. She is adept at weaving together mind, body, and spirit to create a unique environment where profound healing can occur. To accomplish this, she draws on her wealth of experience as a professional, a teacher and therapist, a wife and mother, and generously shares from all areas of her life.

A sought-after speaker in her field, Suzanne inspires healthcare providers all over the world to stay energized using her life-changing tools for stress management and full body presence. She also has authored numerous articles, and thousands visit her popular blog, *Presence Matters: Reflections on Body, Mind and Spirit* at http://massagemag.com/massage-blog/presence-matters. She has a private practice in Reston, VA where her clients also benefit from the techniques she teaches. Many of the skills she is known for are in this book.

You can learn more at:
www.HealingFromTheCore.com